A Hunter's Year

Also by Dan Prusi

Country Boy – Adventures from an Untroubled Childhood
A Hunter's Journey – The Education of an Outdoorsman

A Hunter's Year

Dan Prusi

Beaver's Pond Press, Inc.

To My Children
Benjamin, Daniel, Tara, and Ivan

ISBN 1-59298-003-1

Library of Congress Catalog Number: 2003106922

Cover Photos: Dan Prusi
Cover design by Dan Prusi and Linda Walters
Typesetting by Linda Walters, Optima Graphics, Appleton, WI

Printed in the United States of America

First Printing: June 2003

06 05 04 03 02 6 5 4 3 2 1

Published by Beaver's Pond Press, Inc.
7104 Ohms Lane, Suite 216
Edina, MN 55439-2140
(952) 829-8818
www.beaverspondpress.com

Beaver's Pond Press, Inc.

Contents

Acknowledgements

My thanks to the many members of my family, and to the friends, who helped with the preparation of this book. Audrey Wright, Naomi Harju, Sue Johnson and Bill Tuominen all labored through the first draft when there was no polish on the text. Butch Lakanen, and Alex Chisholm read it again and added more polish. I am in their debt.

My wife, Sherilee, the "Alpha Female," has been beside me during the writing of this book and for the last twenty-nine years. Nearly all of my worldly accomplishments have been realized because of her constant support and companionship. It takes patience to be married to a dedicated outdoorsman. Now she has the added burden of being married to a writer. My children have offered encouragement and support throughout, for which I am grateful.

My thanks to all.

Introduction

There are many components to a hunting season, or even a hunt, and many ways to measure its success. People who do not hunt might assume that hunters must take some quantity of their quarry to consider a hunt successful. Certainly hunters enjoy taking game and enjoy the rare hunts where a limit of birds or an exceptional trophy is taken. But there are so many other ingredients that make for a rewarding hunt. There are old friendships that are rekindled each year during the hunting season and new friendships that are born and nurtured. There is the never-ending beauty of the natural world. There is the tradition of being taught by a mentor, usually an older family member, and of passing your knowledge down to the younger or less experienced hunter. In doing that, we get to share a little of their excitement and relive the feelings we had when the sport was new to us. One great appeal of the hunt is that each outing can turn into one of those unforgettable memories we hold so dear.

The 2001/2002 hunting season was, for me, an unforgettable one. It was not a year of outstanding trophies or of particularly heavy game bags. Nonetheless, it was as satisfying as any I have experienced. I hunted duck in three states and deer in two. I walked again—for the first time in almost thirty years—the ground where I learned about hunting. In doing so, I got to hunt with some of the men who helped me learn about the sport. I was able to pass on a bit of the tradition to some younger, less experienced outdoorsmen. As always, I got to marvel at the sunrise over a marsh or woodlot.

This story, this almanac, began as a record of that season. It was originally titled "The Better Half of Year." Shortly after I began writing it, I realized I needed to write about the rest of the year. Otherwise, I might shortchange my theme of the fall hunting season being for me, and many others, the best part of our year. Was I thinking I had to tell people March through August was a boring or unhappy time? On the contrary. For the outdoorsman, the entire year is full of opportunity. A year in nature is a progression of wonders, and the entire cycle of the year is in itself a wonder. For the outdoorsman, or outdoors "person," each month, each day, has much to offer. For the hunter, the hunting season is the climax of the cycle. It is the harvest time. We have an urgent need to take part in it. Therefore, it seemed the completion of this story had to be delayed so the rest of the year could be included as well. The off-season is, in fact, one component of the hunt.

In much of this book, the setting is my home property or areas very close to it. My part of the world is Cedar Valley Township, St. Louis County, Minnesota. It is low, flat country that was cleared of virgin timber in the early 1900s. There are miles of bog and swamp, and the higher areas are covered with aspen, birch and balsam fir. Though certainly not the most picturesque landscape in the state, it—like every wild place—provides things needed by the diverse wildlife that God placed on this earth. There are the common neighbors like deer and raccoon, and less common species like the timber wolf, fisher and moose. For them and for me, this is home, and I consider myself fortunate to have such neighbors.

So here is the story—the story of that hunting season, and the off-season—with a sprinkling of memories from long ago and not so long ago.

It is not the killing that brings satisfaction; it is the contest of skill and cunning. The true hunter counts his achievement in proportion to the effort involved and the fairness of the sport.

Saxton Pope, **Hunting with Bow and Arrow**

September

In the minds of most people, the arrival of September marks the end of summer. In reality, the month can be very summer-like, at least in its first days. There will be some color shown in the leaves by September 1, but many of the trees in this part of the world that have early changing leaves will put on no color show. The balsam poplar and black ash are the species I notice first, but I look for them. The leaves turn brown and are unspectacular. The balsam poplar seems to change regardless of the temperature. The ash will go brown at the very first frost. Still, seventy-degree temperatures and clouds of hungry mosquitoes sometimes make it seem like autumn is a long way off. We who love the crisp autumn air will long for a frost or two. By month's end, our wish is often granted, for the first killing frost will sometimes arrive during September. The mosquitoes will be gone then, and I will be relieved.

Numbers of songbirds have already left the area. Others are now in large flocks in readiness for migration. Regardless of the temperature, birds and animals will be following their seasonal routines. Many, perhaps all, take their cues from the decreasing amount of daylight. The whitetail bucks may begin the month with velvet on their antlers, but will shed that velvet before October arrives. Grouse broods will still be together on Labor Day, but when autumn officially begins, later in the month, they will be scattered.

Until very recently, September 1 was the day Minnesota hunters could take to the field each year. The seasons on woodcock and black bear traditionally opened on this date until the numbers of those little "buzz bombs"—the woodcock—started to plummet and the state wisely lowered the bag limit and shortened the season. For bear, however, things went in the complete opposite direction. Their population has done very well, and in 2001 Minnesota hunters could begin their hunts in August and take two bear per license. I was not hunting bear in 2001; otherwise, I would have been tending bait stations. The years I do not have a permit for bear, I usually begin my hunting season with a bit of woodcock hunting, just because that is all there is to hunt. In 2001, the "delayed" woodcock season opener coincided with the grouse and archery deer openers. Both of those sports are higher on my priority list. While the grouse numbers were down from the previous two years, my prospects for archery deer season looked very good.

Back Forty Bow Hunt

Our property has been managed for wildlife for a number of years, and for the last several years, with an emphasis on waterfowl. Of course, this involves creating ponds. Each time we excavate a pond we seed the newly exposed earth with the seeds of plants that are preferred by deer. On our little seventy-seven acre parcel there is a mosaic of ponds, sloughs, timber and openings. The openings have also been seeded with clover and other plants that draw in the deer. In addition to this, our neighbor's properties are good habitat, by design or by accident, putting our land in the middle of a large block of good to excellent autumn deer habitat. Our deer herd had suffered terrible losses in the early '90s, caused by several consecutive winters of deep snow and bitter cold. The Minnesota Department of Natural Resources, whose job it is to manage this herd, cut back on antler-less permits for several years in an effort to reduce the harvest. We also got lucky with three consecutive mild winters leading up to the 2001 season. Deer were everywhere in our neighborhood and in good numbers. I spent much of my free time walking the network of trails that crisscross the property. Here I had seen seven different bucks, along with many does and fawns. None of these were trophy bucks, but there were a couple with decent six-point racks and at least two fork-horns. Spike bucks were just about everywhere you looked.

Naturally, seeing so many deer, and so many bucks, was keeping me anxious for the upcoming archery season. Besides the prospect of abundant game, my brother-in-law, Roger, was planning to bow hunt with me. That added to my excitement, for Roger has been a favorite hunting partner over the years. He had not bow hunted for several seasons, and this year he was planning to dust off his gear and give it another try. Roger is one of those rare individuals who seems perpetually cheerful, and is always good company. To hunt with an old buddy adds a lot to any outing.

We got together before the season so I could get him familiar with which trails the deer had been using, and we spent a day setting up several portable tree stands. It felt much like years before when he, I and the rest of our group, were awfully dedicated bow hunters.

I began bow hunting in 1977 along with two of my brothers-in-law. I was lucky that first year. I killed a nice doe seven days into the season, and experienced many exciting encounters. I learned a lot about deer and was hooked on hunting with bow and arrow. Over the years, several friends and relatives joined our original threesome, and for almost twenty years, the archery deer season was the high point of my year and the focus of my hunting energy. We shot a lot of arrows in the off-season and one year set up a field course along the trails behind my house. We read Fred Bear's stories and tried all the gadgets. We got to be pretty good at following blood trails. Each year, four to six of us would take a week off and camp out in tents and tent campers, enjoying hard hunting during the days and good company in the evenings.

The campouts were about as much fun as anything I have done outdoors. We began bringing our kids along for the first weekend of the trip. We began a tradition of having a huge breakfast on the last day in camp, for our wives, kids, and other guests. It was known as the "pig-out breakfast" and the menu might feature just about anything, for we cooked up all of our leftover food supplies. During the week we camped, a lot of folks we knew got in the habit of coming out to visit us. I wonder now if we were not some kind of a curiosity. Me in particular, for my comfortable home was only a mile down the road, yet there I was, camping out in weather that sometimes got down to fifteen degrees during the night.

Eventually, several of the fellows from our group purchased the land where we had been camping and built a shack there. About the same time, one of the guys moved away from the area and several of us got busy with "kid's stuff" like sports and scouts. Not long after the shack was built, our weeklong hunting holiday sort of faded away. Most of the group continued to bow hunt, but it was not the hunting "party" it had been for years. I am not sure exactly why, because we are all still great friends. However, the tradition went away. Nevertheless, those years were seasons full of learning as well as good fun and gave me more fond memories than I can count. Memories of game taken, missed shots, and shared moments around the campfire.

Our best success during our "golden years" of archery hunting came while hunting the many farm fields in the neighborhood during the late afternoon and evening. Our area still had several active farms then, and the local farmers would usually have fields where they had planted oats, under-seeded with clover. The oats would be harvested in late August or early September. After the harvest, the clover would put on a burst of growth. The deer would begin feeding on the clover almost immediately, to take advantage of the high protein available in the new growth. This first flurry of feeding on the fields had often passed by the time archery season began. However, the newly seeded fields were still attractive to the animals. Generally, deer used them every evening and during the night. Later, as the weather cooled and we experienced the first frosts of autumn, the amount of high protein food in the woodlands steadily decreased. The deer would then again turn to the clover fields, with renewed intensity, for their nutrition.

The hunting was good. I killed seventeen deer with my bow the first seventeen seasons I hunted. All but three or four were taken from evening stands. My partners also got most of their deer from evening stands on these fields. Naturally, the best time of the evening watch was the very end of the day, so we got very used to tracking our deer at night with the aid of flashlights or gas lanterns. It was one of the things we all enjoyed the most. Following a faint blood trail into the thickets—at night—was like entering another world. Each step might bring you to the downed animal, or you might jump it from its bed. It was high suspense in the crisp autumn air, sometimes accompanied by owls hooting and the distant wail of a coyote.

I was the only one of the group that lived in the area we hunted. I got to hunt weekday evenings a lot more than the others did, and my pals often got calls for help from me during the week, to track an arrowed deer. They nearly always dropped whatever they were doing to come lend a hand. We had many such episodes that lasted into the wee hours of the morning. Many times, we would give up for a portion of the night, and then return to the trail at first light. We lost more deer than I like to think about, but the huge majority of our tracking adventures ended with the deer found and a small celebration, held wherever the trail had led us.

In January of 1996, I got my first bird dog. She was a golden retriever named Jill. I got her mainly for waterfowl hunting but also trained her for upland work. She did a good job with both types of hunting. I was getting into waterfowling, and hunting upland with Jill for grouse and woodcock was a real pleasure. These activities began to take up more and more of my free time, and more and more of my tree stand and deer-scouting time was sacrificed to spend time with the dog, either hunting or training. I still bow hunted every year, but spent fewer and fewer hours at it. I went several years without filling my archery tag. You need to be out there a lot to be consistently successful. The hours spent scouting are as important, or more important, than the stand time. In 2001, though, the prospects for bow hunting looked to be the best I had seen in many years.

I hunted alone for most of the opening weekend and saw just a few deer. I had no shooting opportunities. For many years, I had passed up shooting does and had even passed on a number of small bucks. Now, after going several years without a deer, I was unsure each day I hunted as to whether I would let anything walk by me without trying a shot. I was pretty sure I would pass up a doe. However, anything with horns and in decent range was probably going to have an arrow sent its way. I had my opportunity on the fourth day of the season.

That afternoon, Roger came out for a hunt. He picked me up at the house and we drove to the field at the south end of my property. We parked a couple of hundred yards from the county road. From there, Roger walked in another quarter-mile to a portable stand we had set up during the pre-season. I told Roger I would take a short walk, through the center of the property, to check for deer sign. I would then take a stand in one of the many portables we had set up. I followed one of the walking trails, heading north, and spent perhaps twenty minutes checking out the sign near several stands. I decided I would hunt a portable, set up alongside one of the dikes that also served as a roadway rimming one of the ponds. We had seen deer there often, and they were feeding regularly on the clover growing there. I had kept this area mowed all summer, and the clover thrives when mowed now and again. The stand was set up in a small group of four trees. The trees stood by themselves, where one trail met another. I had placed stands here many times over the years. It was not what I would call a "lucky" stand. In fact, from this exact location, several years earlier, I ended a significant streak of consecutive hits. I had blown an excellent opportunity at a nice fork buck. Nonetheless, this was a good place to catch a deer, either traveling the roadway or feeding on the abundant clover.

I had barely settled into the stand, no more than five minutes off the ground, when I spotted a deer. To the north, at the far side of the small pond, a deer walked out of the alders and onto the spoil bank. It was a spike buck. He began to follow the bank around the pond towards me, stopping to take an occasional nibble from the ground. I was quite sure he would come right to me, for he was on an area of uncut vegetation. The wild grasses that grew there were generally not as appealing as the mowed clover areas, such as I had right below the stand. I thought it likely he would move quickly along to get to this patch of more appealing food. This he did. I had a brief discussion with myself as to whether I should take a shot at this non-trophy. I quickly talked myself into taking a shot if the deer came within fifteen yards and offered the proper angle. It took only a few minutes for him to do just that.

He was only ten yards from me when he stopped to feed on the clover. He was quartering slightly towards me but nearly broadside. It was an extremely quiet evening, and I knew the slightest noise would get his attention. I let him feed for a little while to settle him down but I didn't dare wait too long. If he decided to keep moving along the roadway, he would be out of my shooting area quickly. I raised the bow. As I did, he must have heard something, for his head came up and he looked directly at me. I froze. I wish I had a dollar for every time I have been in this situation—where a worried deer stares you in the face and you have to remain motionless in hopes it will mistake you for a part of the landscape.

I was wearing camo of course, and I had cut a pile of balsam boughs when I set up the stand and hung them behind it to prevent me from being skylined. I was glad I had done so now, because the deer watched me for only a little while, and then went back to feeding. As I began my draw, I held the bow at a sharp, downward angle, due to the deer being so close to the stand. Because of this, the string came to rest against my left leg, long before I could reach full draw. I had to move my leg to allow the string to clear, and this got me another quick glance from the buck. Thankfully, it was a brief glance, for now I was at full draw. As soon as the buck resumed feeding, I bent at the waist and lowered my bow down. I was almost on target, but still the string was hitting my leg. Now the buck began to raise his head again. I let the arrow go.

I am always amazed at how quickly a deer can react to the sound of a twanging bowstring. Frequently, especially if the animal is nervous, it will react to the sound of the arrow being released and launch itself into flight. I know a fellow who once shot an arrow at a deer and the animal had completely swapped ends by the time the arrow arrived, taking the shaft in the opposite side the shooter had aimed for. More often, the arrow arrives before the deer can spring away, but not before the animal has "bunched" himself up in preparation for that first bound. When that happens, his body drops considerably towards the ground. That spot you picked out on the deer can be a foot lower than it was when you released. On this occasion, my target did that "bunching up" and was quite a lot lower when the arrow got there. I had aimed higher than I would have liked, and the arrow went higher than I thought I had aimed. The string may also have been on my leg, which could have affected the shot. On the other hand, I might have just made a very bad shot. At any rate, the arrow just missed the top of the buck's back and buried itself into the ground as he spun and then took two or three jumps in the direction he had come from.

This deer was no genius. He stopped less than thirty yards from me and began to look around trying to figure out what had happened. He looked nervously here and there, and each time he glanced away from me, I would move a little in an attempt to get another arrow from the quiver onto the string. It wasn't often I had pulled that trick off, but this time I somehow managed to do it. The deer was nervous, but came in again and began to feed. I now had a chance of getting a second shot, and while most of the time that does not happen, it is not all that unusual. Over the years, I have occasionally managed to get multiple shots (and misses) at the same deer. At least twice, one of my partners has left their stand with their quiver empty!

The buck now chose a different spot to feed in, and he was much more nervous than he had been a few minutes before. Nevertheless, he began munching away twelve yards from me. He was now quartering away too sharply for a good shot, so I waited for a while. He finally turned enough to present a decent shot. I drew and let go another arrow.

This time the deer really jumped the string, and the arrow hit him at the front of the hindquarter with a loud whack. I instantly had the sick feeling that comes after a bad shot placement. Flashbacks reminded me of the times we spent a long night and part of the next day trying unsuccessfully to recover a wounded deer. It is a most unpleasant feeling. But to my surprise, after a single leap, the buck stopped and then spun in a circle. After a pause of a half-second, he made another circle, not trying to move away from me at all. He stood for a second as I got a third arrow ready. Then he slowly lay down, facing away from me. He was obviously hit hard, and now my mind tried to process the current information and decide whether to shoot yet again. I had no good opening for another shot, so I watched for a few seconds wondering what the deer would do.

It is hard for me to judge time in such situations. It may be I am so full of adrenaline, time becomes distorted. If I had to guess, I would say it was ten or fifteen seconds after he lay down when I saw his head start to lower. I knew then he was finished. I attached my lift rope to the bow, lowered it to the ground, unbuckled my safety belt and climbed down to the ground. He was dead before I got there.

I had ended a long dry spell. It was an especially long dry spell with my bow. I felt satisfaction, both in ending the drought and in securing some venison. Still, I was not terribly excited. The buck was not much of a trophy. But I had taken him fairly and he would be terrific on the table. I also felt great relief that, in spite of a poor shot, the deer had gone down and died very quickly. I would also now be able to concentrate on the opening of duck season without fretting over whether I should deer hunt.

I gutted the animal where he lay and walked back to the house. I got in the pickup and drove right up to the animal, taking a wide drive around where Roger was sitting. I thought there was no reason to bother him for help, as he still had ninety minutes or so of shooting light. I got the deer loaded up and drove back out. As I again entered the field where Roger was posted, I saw he was out of the stand and on his way over to me. I stopped the truck and told him I had things under control and that he could have stayed in his stand. He said once he knew I had a deer, he was too excited to stay put.

He had not seen me get into my stand, so he had not been sure where I was. He had seen the buck when it came out near the pond and watched it as it walked along the edge of the pond. After a few moments, the buck had passed out of his sight. Then he heard the "whack" of my arrow hitting but was not sure what the noise was. A few minutes later, he saw me, first standing on the ground and then kneeling down. When I stood up and again knelt down, he knew I had scored.

I told him my story and accepted his enthusiastic congratulations. When the "kill talk" was over, we took a short walk around the field. I showed him some well-used deer trails leading into the field. He decided he would stay at the field, and hunt until dark. I drove on out and got the deer home, where I washed out the body cavity and prepared the deer for hanging. Roger was in for more excitement that evening.

He moved to a permanent stand in an oak tree, just 100 yards from the portable where he had first set up that evening. He had barely settled in when a six-point buck, accompanied by a smaller buck, appeared right under the stand where he had been just a half-hour earlier. The deer fed towards him and as they got close, the stillness of the evening was such that he could hear them pulling up the clover as they fed. Having been in many situations like this, I can imagine the excitement Roger was feeling. Because of the bow hunter's need to be very close to the quarry, we experience things the rifle hunter often does not. Watching two undisturbed bucks, feeding calmly towards you while you can actually hear them chewing, is exciting to the point where a fellow can easily come unglued.

It was not long before my partner got a chance at one of the bucks, broadside at twenty yards. His shot missed, and just as my deer had done, this one took a few jumps and stopped. The second buck then presented a chance. In fact, it stood in the exact spot where the first had been. Roger missed this second buck as well. He then managed to get a second shot at one of them. As he tried to get arrow number four out of his quiver, both bucks walked right under him and into the field. By the time he was ready for another shot, they were out at over thirty yards. He declined to shoot. The deer eventually fed out of sight. Roger came to the house after staying on stand until the end of legal shooting hours.

He was excited and a little down on himself for missing these chances. He said when he missed that first perfect chance, he had thought to himself he might have to hunt a long time to get another opportunity that good. When he got two more chances within minutes, he could hardly believe it. This goes to show how unpredictable a hunt can be.

My own bow hunting for the year was done, but Roger came out for several more hunts and had even more opportunities. He ended up missing more shots. In all, he had six shots at three or four different bucks. When he did not hunt the last part of the season, I teased him a little, saying he quit just when the odds were beginning to swing in his favor. The teasing is fun to do when your venison is in the freezer. You know it will be a whole year before you have an opportunity to be on the other end of the teasing.

Archery hunting for me in 2001 was abbreviated, but when it is abbreviated by success, it is not hard to take. Still, many hours in a deer stand, watching the leaves changing colors and falling throughout the season, feeling the wind on your face, and enjoying the colors of sunrise and sunset, are all hours well spent. Fortunately, I could experience these things again during the upcoming duck and firearms deer seasons.

Hunt 'em Up

After two excellent seasons, our grouse numbers were down in 2001. The bird population had crashed and the birds were few and far between. My constant companion in pursuit of grouse or ducks is my dog, Jill. She loves the upland bird work because she is active almost every moment of the hunt, whereas with waterfowl she relies on me to bring in the occasional duck and knock it down. I don't always hold up my end too well. However, with upland work, she can use her own skills to get herself a taste of feathers. At times, she hasn't even had to rely on my shooting, for she has managed to catch grouse at least a half-dozen times, without me firing a shot. On one of those occasions, she also made me look like a "wise ol' woodsman." That day, I was hunting with a young friend. It was cool and a steady drizzle was coming down. As we approached an area covered with balsam fir trees, I told my companion this was an area likely to have birds on a day like this. Grouse often seek the cover provided by the thick boughs of balsam stands during a rain. The words were barely out of my mouth when Jill, who had been quartering in front of us in her search for birds, emerged from the balsam trees with a live grouse in her mouth.

While the grouse were few that fall of 2001, Jill and I still went out in search of them. Our best hunt of the season came during its first week, on an evening hunt. The foliage was still thick and green for the most part, and such conditions make the shooters job more difficult. I know people who don't even begin their grouse hunting until the leaves have fallen a bit. For me, it is hard enough to wait for the open season, much less to wait for conditions to improve. Leaves or no leaves, good grouse counts or bad, I had pursued these wonderful game birds with some measure of dedication since I was twelve. After thirty-five years, that measure of dedication has lessened, but I think I will be looking for grouse to shoot at for many years, if my body allows. This lessening of the passion for a certain pursuit is common in sportsmen, though a true love will never go away. A man I occasionally duck hunt with in Arkansas summed it up well for me one day as he tried to describe why he no longer duck hunts every day of the open season. He said, "I'm not mad at 'em like I used to be."

So, in spite of thick, green foliage and not much prospect of running into many birds, Jill and I set out on our first serious grouse hunt of the season. It was early evening. I carried my grouse and woodcock gun, the old Ithaca model 37 I had inherited from my dad. It is a light gun, and short barreled. I had had the adjustable choke removed and the barrel reworked to accept a screw-in choke. Improved cylinder is my choice for grouse and woodcock, and it serves nicely on decoying ducks as well. Grouse and woodcock hunting require the hunter to be quick on the draw, and the weight and barrel length on the Ithaca allow me to be just a little quicker than some other guns might.

Jill had done the "bounce" when I donned my upland vest, put the whistle lanyard around my neck and picked up the shotgun. She springs into the air over and over again, panting, as I get ready to leave. As we move out of the yard, she races far ahead and then back to my side, anxious to begin the hunt. Sometimes it takes us a little while to settle her down. It is difficult to keep her in as close as I would like her to be. Especially at the beginning of a hunt, the excitement combines with her well-rested condition to put her into high gear. I can't be too upset with her, for all of her faults I lay at the feet of her trainer, who had never trained a bird dog before. Me.

We would not work the thick cover this evening. I should say that I would not work the thick cover. As abundant as the leaves were, it would be almost impossible for me to get a shot there. However, I could walk the trails and the edges of the brush, and Jill was happy to work within that jungle. It would largely be a matter of luck as to whether I got a shot at any birds she flushed, depending entirely on what route the bird would take. It would also be

harder to "read" the dog. "Reading" the dog means the hunter needs to watch his dog to see how it is behaving. When they find the scent of a bird, their posture and behavior changes. The hunter has at least some warning that there may be a bird nearby. Jill is a flushing dog, but I really believe I could have taught her to point. When she comes upon a stationary bird, she will pause and look back to me, as if to let me know the bird is there.

I walked the trails and Jill zigzagged back and forth in front of me. The bell on her collar was tinkling and letting me know where she was, for the thick cover prevented me from tracking her visually. The trails run through some areas of young aspen trees standing close beside each other. Such thick sapling stands make excellent grouse and woodcock cover, for here, their winged enemies, the hawks and owls, cannot easily negotiate. Fifteen minutes into the hunt, I heard the whir of grouse wings from near the sound of the tinkling bell. At the flush the bell stopped, as the dog obviously stopped to watch the bird fly off. It had flushed from perhaps thirty yards away, and I couldn't really determine what direction it had flown other than that it had not come towards me. Rather than guess which way it had gone, I called to Jill and indicated to her, with hand signals, to continue to hunt along the trail.

She was not doing badly, needing only an occasional caution from me with voice or whistle, to come in closer. We came to what we call the Bear Country Pond and walked the dike that runs between the pond and a large slough. I hoped we might run into a pheasant here—one of those I had released for dog training—but I was disappointed. Beyond the dike, there were pockets of woods that often held grouse. I recalled another early season hunt when, in that first pocket, I had heard Jill flush a bird and could tell from the sound it had landed in a tree. They often do when put up by a dog. The leaves were still thick and green on that day as well, and I worked my way towards the sound that indicated where the bird might be. After making my way twenty yards or so into the woods, I saw Jill. She was standing on a fallen log that was lying across other fallen logs. The top of her perch was three feet or more above the ground, and she was staring right at me. When my eyes met hers, she held the gaze for a second or two, then turned her head, and looked up. There was the grouse, fifteen feet above her. He was perched on a limb, as I have seen many treed grouse, his neck extended and his body feathers flattened, looking long and lean. When I moved in with gun ready, he flushed, and my second shot folded him up. That bird was mostly credited to Jill. Each time she pulls off one of these almost supernatural hunting tricks, I am in awe of what this little hunting dog of mine is able to accomplish.

Today there were no birds to be found in this little niche. We continued on, working more little corners that experience had shown me were preferred by the birds, but none of them gave us any hopeful signs, much less birds. A small flock of mallards jumped up from the slough, but the duck season was still a few weeks away. I walked the edge of the backfield, and Jill crisscrossed alongside of me. We came to the new road that connected two of my fields, and again I prepared myself for a flush. The clover on this road had been attracting some birds. Jill worked first the north side and then the south. I walked the road in an easterly direction. Suddenly, Jill made a sharp turn to her right, nose down, and her tail began to whip back and forth. She was "getting birdy." With the fresh scent of game in her nose, her body quivered with excitement and her moves were quick and purposeful. I heard the flush, and it sounded as if the bird had treed not far off the road. With gun ready, I moved closer. Then came another whir of wings as the bird thought better of his hiding spot in the tree and chose instead to take flight. Its first mistake was to fly towards the opening of the road. An even bigger mistake was to turn straight down that road when he reached the opening. The bird was giving me an opportunity for a shot grouse hunters rarely see. This grouse was in a wide-open lane and going nearly straight away. I had been ready for the flush. He came down in a shower of feathers, making a thump as he hit the hard packed road.

Jill was on him in a flash. She did her usual, rather irritating routine, of picking the bird up and putting him down several times. Each time she put it down she would sort of shake her head and spit out some loose feathers. Again, the failures of her trainer bothered me a little, for a retriever really needs to get on that bird, pick it up and bring it immediately and directly to her handler. But we had a grouse. He was a brown phase male, and as I always do, I spread the tail feathers and admired the subtle beauty of this wonderful bird. The color phases of grouse are not apparent to those who do not see them up close. From a dark red color to gray—and all shades in between—might be seen on grouse that are all from the same area. I hope one day to take a mature bird with the full red color. I have seen only a few of these, where even the "ruff" on the neck, usually shiny black, is a beautiful, iridescent red. I praised Jill, and her attitude told me she was pleased with her own performance. I like to think she was pleased with me, but I don't really know.

We continued along the road. Here we might find grouse, woodcock or pheasant. We found another grouse, this time on my left. As usual, it was Jill who actually found it. Again, the bird flushed into a tree. Like the first, it then changed its mind and took flight. A tougher shot this time. The bird was only a gray-brown flash, moving through the tops of the alders and crossing rather than going away. Somehow, my shot brought it down. This time Jill brought the bird quickly to me. It seems that if she cannot see me, she will be more diligent in picking up the bird and starting towards me. When I am in sight, she starts to dawdle and rearrange the bird in her mouth. Perhaps she thinks she has done enough when she has the bird where I can see it and is hoping I will walk over to get it from her.

We had two grouse in the game pouch, and it felt good to have a little weight back there. I had not expected a pair of birds. Now I let myself think we might come home with four. Perhaps, even a limit of five. I quickly came to my senses and told myself that two was fine. We would start hunting our way back towards the house. It was a quarter-mile away, and we hunted our way back without flushing a bird.

The hunt had given us three flushes and two birds. When back at the house, I looked up a journal entry from 1999. It describes a short evening hunt that had taken place just two miles from my place. It was quite a shoot.

September 28, 1999

After work, I had a quick bite and ran the garbage to the pickup site, then drove to Marty's for a bird hunt. Jill was keyed up. She has had an up and down season, having some of the best performances of her life and some poor ones too. Initially she was super, and then went downhill for a bit when the excitement of the feathers got to her, and has now been improving a bit each time out. We had hunted a little on nine consecutive days and had seven grouse and one woodcock before this hunt.

We started down the logging road and she worked pretty well. After fifteen minutes, we flushed a doodle twice, but no shots. A short time later, I saw her get very birdy and let her work the heavy hazel brush. She put up a grouse that gave me a tough long shot that I missed. We went after it, it flushed from a tree, I rushed the first shot, just plain blew the second, and we were unable to put it up again. We continued to work our way towards the power line. Near the "Y" she put up another bird that I saw but not until it was out of range. Then, near the first landing, she got very birdy and I let her go and tried to keep up. Three different birds got up on the right side of the landing from the raspberry bushes, none giving me a shot. I could tell by watching Jill that the birds had been all around that landing. At the far side, as we were about to re-enter the logging road, she jumped into the berry stalks. She put one up that gave me a straightaway shot I connected on, but the bird still flew so I shot it a second time. Jill retrieved it and worked the brush some more but no more birds got up. We continued down the logging road and Jill seemed birdy the whole time, stayed close, and paid attention to me. A woodcock got up and went straight down the road and my second shot dumped it.

Jill was now really bearing down. Not just fired up, but fired up and working hard and diligently. She didn't fly back and forth but worked slowly and thoroughly. At the next landing, we jumped one that fell at my first shot. Then another jumped that I missed. Jill fetched the downed bird and continued to scour the berry bushes. Another bird got up and landed in a tree. I took two steps towards it, it flushed and I hit it with two consecutive shots, bringing it down. Another retrieve and we raced the fading light to get to another raspberry area. We jumped one other bird on the way there, but flushed no others before darkness caught us. I kept the dog at heel and walked out with a heavy game bag.

This was probably the best Jill and I have ever worked together. I shot reasonably well, and she worked really well. It was as if getting that first bird showed her she should work close and thoroughly and then, we could score as a team. It was great.

That hunt was one of the rare days when man and dog worked in an almost perfect partnership, and each did their job well. Days like that do not come often, for sometimes conditions will not allow it. Birds can be lacking or the scenting conditions can be difficult. I have my bad days shooting and Jill has her bad days working birds. When it all comes together though, it is something you do not soon forget.

We made several other hunts during September 2001, but I believe we only came home with one other grouse and a couple of woodcock. The single hunt described in the 1999 journal entry, which lasted only a few hours, produced more birds for us than the entire 2001 season. This is hunting. We were in the lowest part of the cyclic fluctuation of the grouse population, and most likely, there will be four or five slim years ahead for grouse hunters. I remember as a lad, new to hunting these wonderful birds, how disappointing it was to learn we were in one of the low population time periods and how long four years seemed like it was going to take. Now, thirty-five years or more after killing my first grouse, I know they will eventually be back. They will be back in great numbers. I know I won't suffer to any great degree while I wait. There are so many other things to do while the grouse population builds! When it does, and the coveys once again fill the raspberry patches, I hope I am able to devote many hours to pursuing these exciting birds.

October

October is a month of great change. In my area of Minnesota, it is often the transition month from autumn to winter. We may have beautiful Indian Summer weather that can occur any time during the month, and on occasion, the first blasts of winter visit us near month's end. Not many years ago, my weeklong bow hunting vacation was cut short by thirty-six inches of snow that fell the last two days of the month. One cannot count on the Indian Summer, or on the snowstorms, but it is almost certain October will have many of the days that, for me, are the best God makes. I am talking about the clear and frosty mornings when the ground is covered in white, and the frozen grass and clover crunch beneath your feet. Footprints made on such a day can often be seen for the rest of the fall. These are the mornings when you are anxious for the sun to get above the horizon. Both for the beautiful view you will have of morning sunshine on the frosty landscape, and for the warmth those first rays of sunshine bring to you. The skim ice appears on the edges of the streams and perhaps covers over the still water ponds. The air is fresh and clear. You know that by noon, you may feel like napping in some sunny opening.

The month begins with the beautiful colors of autumn, but it is not long before the trees have shed their leaves. The stands of deciduous trees look brown and gray, except on the forest floor where those leaves lie scattered. Some of our birds have left us for the season, including some of the blue-winged teal. I wish these would tarry just a bit, so we might have a chance at them, come duck season.

October is hunting season and you know each day might become one you will never forget. The cover thins with the falling leaves. There may be more and better shots at grouse and northern ducks may appear at any time. The bucks will begin their first rutting movement of the year and perhaps give you an opportunity September seldom offers. It is, without doubt, the best month of the best half of year.

This Corner of the World

Almost twenty years ago, my wife and I purchased sixty-seven acres of land that adjoined the ten acres we already owned. This little corner of the world is the setting for much of this book, so I think I should tell you a bit more about it.

When we bought the land there were three farmed fields— each from seven to ten acres in size—and the rest of the property was wooded. The forested land included a small cedar swamp, a nice stand of black ash, a very thick alder swamp, and the rest was covered with balsam fir, aspen and balsam poplar. It is quite flat and much of it is rather swampy. A tiny watercourse cuts through the northwest corner. It was not then, nor is it now, the most beautiful piece of ground in the world or even in the township. But it is ours, and like just about every piece of ground, it is home to many kinds of wildlife. Since we bought it, much time and energy has been invested in making it a better home for our wild neighbors.

I always dreamed of owning property and improving it for wildlife. I put that dream aside and filed it far away among those dreams I thought had little chance of coming true. When we were able to acquire the additional acreage, many long dormant ideas and plans sprang to life. I had a lot more plans than I did time or money. Fortunately, with financial assistance from several public agencies, even a man of my modest means was able to make many improvements to the land. The very first year we built a small pond and planted food plots for deer. Over the next several years, we planted thousands of trees. We did a limited amount of logging that generated a bit of cash, and this logging regenerated our aspen trees. When an area is logged with the clear-cut method (removing nearly all the trees) and there are even just a few aspen among the trees that are removed, the aspen root systems send up thousands of new shoots. You have a new aspen stand on its way. These young aspen stands are valuable habitat components for deer, grouse, rabbit and woodcock. Many non-game species also use these younger stands of trees. Clear-cutting has a bad connotation among many folks, but the clear-cuts we did were never more than an acre in size. We also spread this logging activity out over time, in order to have some of this young aspen growth included in our little "wildlife park" for several years.

I built nest boxes like mad and placed them all around the property. There were probably 150 of these erected over the years. Birds and small mammals, ranging in size from the tiny wren to the mighty great horned owl, have used them. I am a meticulous note taker. For many years, I recorded the types of birds and animals that used the boxes. I knew how many eggs and young birds came out of each. It was a wonderful experience to learn such things and to learn them through observation and experience, rather than by reading a book or research paper. I did the reading too, and it helped to round out my education. I enjoy reading, and to supplement that study with hands-on experience made this the most pleasant of my educational experiences. It is great fun to find the first bluebird nest built in one of the boxes I made with bluebirds in mind. In recent years, I have only recorded the use of my wood duck boxes, which number about twenty-five. While I no longer record data for the other nest boxes, I still maintain several dozen of them in addition to the duck boxes.

The most significant changes we have made to the landscape are the ponds and wetlands we have built. As mentioned, the land is low and swampy. If you scrape a little soil out of the ground, our high water table insures that it will be a pond. Small dikes, strategically placed, can flood a fair bit of area when the landscape is as flat as ours is, and we have taken advantage of this. We have tried

many things and done them many different ways.

Our first pond, now known as "Old Pond," is a simple sixty-foot by ninety-foot rectangle. It was designed by the Soil Conservation Service. These folks worked with me on several projects as well as provided funds. When it was first built, I was like a kid with a new toy, walking out to observe the wildlife around it every chance I got. A few years later, I designed another excavated pond and ran the plan by the Soil Conservation Service folks. They liked it, so it was built, followed by two others. Now, in addition to Old Pond, we had Big Pond, Cedar Pond and Bear Country Pond. Then came the slough and the L Pond, and my wife began to hint we had too many ponds. In order to appease her, I brought in a dozer and converted several of the ponds into one contiguous wetland. Funny, that was not what she had in mind.

So how many ponds do we have? Well that depends on what you count as a pond. I guess there are eight or nine. Nothing very large, but when we bought the place we had zero acres of waterfowl habitat, and now there are about ten acres suitable for nesting waterfowl. Nest they did. During our best year of brood production, we had eighty-seven young wood ducks and hooded mergansers leave the boxes. In addition, there were broods of ground nesting mallards and teal. Not bad for just a few acres, especially considering that until we began managing for waterfowl, no ducks were hatching on this ground.

A few years back, the land north of, and adjacent to ours, was sold. The man who purchased it also enjoyed building ponds. He quickly turned a brushy, rather ugly piece of ground into what looks like a city park. He built perhaps ten ponds of various sizes and depths and planted grass, clover, and other plants that wildlife love on the banks of these ponds. He keeps more acres mowed than I care to count. His property definitely has a different look than mine. His has a manicured look; mine, a wild look. His ponds look like those on a golf course, mine look like beaver ponds. He is happy and I am happy. The geese love his place and the ducks love mine. He also gets some ducks and I, some geese. What works to everyone's advantage is the fact that from the air, these two properties have to look very attractive to waterfowl passing overhead. If they take the time to drop down for a look, they are bound to find one or two ponds have what they are after, so my own work and that of my neighbor complement each other. The banks of the ponds are full of succulent green plants that the deer love, so we have plenty of them in our area.

Big Pond is only about a half-acre in size and has two small islands. One of these islands has a pair of large tamarack trees and several ash trees on it. The pond was excavated in 1989. The banks were leveled and then seeded to clover. Loafing logs for the muskrats and ducks were set up, and tubers of arrowhead and sago pondweed were planted. A nesting platform for owls was placed in the deformed top of one of the tamarack trees on the island. It is a simple cone of chicken wire, lined with tarpaper and then filled with sticks. Wood duck box Number 1 was nailed to one of the ash trees on the island. In 1999, we constructed a dike at the upstream end of the pond. This flooded about an acre of ground that had scattered ash trees and grassy swamp vegetation growing in it. Two of these ash trees had wood duck houses mounted as well, and another was mounted on a pipe right out in the pond. Big Pond has been a wildlife magnet since it was built.

The first year of Big Pond's existence, I took a nice six-point buck from a stand there as he fed on the clover. When that buck came out to feed, there were two grouse and two rabbits feeding on the clover and two other deer. My son Danny had a close encounter with a monster buck at the same stand a year or two later, but failed to get a shot when the deer sensed danger and doubled back. My cousin also killed a small buck from a stand at Big Pond with his rifle in about 1998. The little island with the trees has had flying squirrels living in the hollow tamarack and both wood ducks and hooded mergansers have nested in the hollows as well. Wood duck box Number 1 was the first box we put up and the first one ever to attract a nesting hen—a hooded merganser—that showed up in 1992. For ten years running, Number 1 hatched merganser broods. One year, after the mergansers were done using the box, a pair of kestrels took it over. They too, successfully raised a brood. In 1998 a pair of great horned owls nested in the platform, raising two young and providing me with hours of fun observing them. I also got videotape and still photos of the young birds in the nest. The owls did not seem to bother the mergansers that were nested less than thirty feet away.

The wood duck boxes in and around Big Pond have the best occupancy rate of any on the property. Three or four of them are always occupied, usually by the little mergansers but wood ducks have also nested there. Herons hunt this pond and in the summer, the bottom is black with tadpoles in all shallow areas. When they have turned from tadpoles to frogs and begin their exodus from the water to dry land, it sometimes seems like the ground is moving. Tiny tree frogs by the tens of thousands have hatched there. Studies on predators show that many of them will rely on whatever food is most available. I can't help but think a steady supply of tree frogs takes a little of the predator pressure off songbirds, and perhaps game birds and animals as well.

One of our more recent projects was to flood about five acres of swampy ground by constructing a dike. The area had been sparsely covered with cedar and I had this logged off before the dike was built. A narrow channel was excavated around the entire perimeter of the slough to provide open water. The interior has shallow water and cattails. It is easy for little critters to hide in this emergent vegetation, and it was after this project was completed that we began to attract wood ducks. I surmise that we finally provided them with proper brood cover where they could safely raise their young. The redwing blackbirds love to nest in cattails and we have had bitterns nesting there. In the late summer and early fall, I see the little birds known as rails running through the shallows. I assume they have nested here.

It is plain to see that, with a little work and planning, one can make a real impact on the landscape and its wildlife. For me, it has been the most satisfying of hobbies. The work continues and it is enjoyable work. Watching the wildlife respond to these offerings gives me a feeling of accomplishment and joy.

On the West Branch

I don't know why, but I came to be a duck hunter rather late in my hunting career. I had hunted waterfowl occasionally since I was about thirteen years old. Not often, but every now and then, someone convinced me to try a duck hunt. I also had tried it on my own a few times while I was still in high school. In about 1992, I suddenly fell in love with the sport. Perhaps I didn't realize what I was missing for the previous twenty-five years. Since that revelation though, ducks and duck hunting have been a passion and my favorite of all the wonderful kinds of hunting.

Minnesota opens its season on the Saturday closest to October 1, so to me, October means ducks. That is not to say I don't do other things in October, because the grouse and archery deer seasons still get my attention during the month. I sometimes do a little trapping as well. However, those are just sideline diversions or, in the case of trapping, a necessary part of my property management. In fact, the trapping is strictly muskrat control. That control is necessary to minimize the little rodent's impact on the wild rice in the ponds and on the dikes that hold the water in the ponds. Even the trapping is done with ducks in mind.

My duck hunting is done almost entirely on small waters near where I live. Most duck hunters in my area of the state hunt divers on the big lakes west of where I live. My hunting grounds are just out of the big flyway to the west and it is tough hunting. I like to hunt over decoys but because of the limited number of birds flying around, decoy shooting is not going to get you many birds. My typical day in the marsh is an early morning decoy hunt followed by paddling around in my canoe or hiking around on my feet, looking for quiet places that might hold the odd duck or two. I am usually alone except for my dog; however, my son-in-law, Derek, and my nephew, Matt, have taken a liking to the sport. They join me now and again, as do other friends. I usually need to tag along with others when I do any serious diver hunting, because my gear is the type used for puddle ducks on small waters. Fortunately, my "network" includes friends with larger boats and plenty of bluebill decoys.

For a number of years, I have opened the duck season on the West Branch of the Floodwood River. West Branch is what we call it. It is a tiny stream that runs south out of Pancake Lake near Wawina. Choked with brush, it winds through some farms and forest and is spanned by a couple of bridges along quiet country roads. It does not look like much of a duck-hunting stream where I put my canoe in near one of these bridges. As you paddle down from this bridge, you leave all signs of habitation quickly behind you. You are never far from people but, except for the occasional sounds of chain saws or tractors, you would think you were. Soon, you come to areas where the beaver have dammed the stream and flooded large areas along its banks. There, you will likely jump your first ducks. Mostly wood ducks and green-winged teal can be found here as well as an occasional mallard. The farther downstream you go the more open water and open marsh you encounter. This is where you will likely see mallards. About forty minutes into your trip downstream, if you are taking it easy with your paddling, you come to a place where an old drainage ditch meets the stream. From this point on, you have a wider stream and much more flooded grass. This is the duck marsh. As you move downstream there will be less and less brush and increasingly open marsh. There are places where higher land, covered with trees and brush, reach out into the marsh. Now, for several miles, the river runs through a sea of cattails and other emergent wetland plants. It stays that way until you meet (after several hours of paddling) the main branch of the Floodwood River.

This junction of the two streams forms a small, shallow lake. In dry years, the lake is more a sea of grass with a narrow channel snaking through it. Where the merged streams leave the lake, the riparian forest begins. River maple and oak line the banks from this point on, and the higher ground has basswood, birch and aspen. While I have hunted the river where it flows through this forest, I most often hunt the upper reaches. The area from where that first manmade ditch joins the river, to the lake, is where I spend many hours each fall.

It is easy to say you know every bend in a river, and I have said that about me and this stretch of water. I had thought that might be an overstatement, but in recent years I have hunted until sunset, while several miles downstream, and paddled back in coal black darkness without ever wondering where I was on the river. The first time this happened, I was amazed at how I knew when to begin a turn to keep inside the main channel. It occurred to me that perhaps this was not unlike what deer and other animals are able to do as they negotiate their territories in storms and darkness. Their familiarity with the escape trails allows them to flee along them without error, no matter what the conditions. At any rate, I know this stretch of river.

This area never holds any great number of ducks. It is mostly local birds that have nested near here, along with their young of the year. Occasionally, northern birds show up to keep the hunting interesting throughout the season. There are enough Canada geese in the area throughout the season that you may get a crack at these great birds any day you are here. The big appeal of this area is that, usually, my companions and I are the only hunters on the river. It has fewer ducks and more solitude than the popular duck hunting areas. That, for me, is ideal.

The previous fall, I tried to improve the habitat by sowing wild rice in some of the shallow pools that lay along the river. Twice I had carried in a couple of five-gallon pails filled with rice when I came in for a duck hunt. I had tossed the seeds out of the canoe in likely looking spots as I paddled here and there. A scouting trip in August revealed the rice had done extremely well, and we saw several broods of young birds in and around the new rice beds. There

were mallards, teal and widgeon families, and all of these were found in the new rice beds. The prospects for opening weekend were good.

On the eve of the season, my daughter and her husband drove up from their home in the big city to stay with us. Tara, my only daughter, is bright, beautiful and perfect in all ways. This is exactly what all "only daughters" are, in their father's eyes. Her husband, Derek, can fix motors and all things automotive. He likes to do chores around my place and he hunts ducks with me. That is exactly three more things than most people expect from a son-in-law. It was easy to see him as one of my children, and would have been even if he did not know how to keep my truck running. On opening day, it would be Derek, my nephew, Matt, my niece's husband, Jake, his brother-in-law, Grant, and me. Our plan was for Jake and Grant to paddle down from the bridge starting at noon. This is our legal start time on opening day. Matt, Derek and I would pull a boat and canoe to the river, with our ATVs, about an hour's paddle below the bridge. I planned to set up the boat in a large pool hidden in willows and rice, while Matt and Derek paddled downstream. The two pairs of hunters in the canoes would jump shoot, and perhaps keep birds moving up and down the river, towards me, and towards each other.

As we unloaded our gear at the road, we met a couple of other hunters who were going to be duck hunting "my" river. I was surprised to learn they had bought land along the access trail I used, and since my scouting trip in August, had built a hunting shack there. They were decent fellows and did not want at all to prevent us from hunting, but just as I would do, they asked where we would be set up. We all wanted to avoid having our parties too close to each other. They eventually set up a short distance upstream from me, and the movement of our hunters in the canoes ended up helping their efforts.

As we set up, there were many ducks in the air. They were mostly mallards, and some of these set their wings to land in our decoys even as we finished setting them up. The adults had not heard the guns for many months. The young birds had never faced a hunter's barrage, and they were tame. By the end of the day, that would change. Just before noon, I sent the boys downstream and it was not long at all until the first shots of the season boomed out along the river bottom. First, the fellows downstream got some shooting. A bit later, so did the upstream crew. Both canoes were jumping birds, both parties in between were getting shots, and there was a fifteen to twenty-minute period of steady action. My shooting this opening day was off just a little. I would rather it had been way off than be the way it was that day, for I hit a lot of ducks that didn't come down. I would much rather miss them than cripple them. I managed to get two mallards.

During that first twenty minutes of intense shooting, Jill had been beside herself with excitement. Normally well behaved and willing to sit quietly until given the command to retrieve, for some reason, she was all over the boat. I was turning this way and that as birds were coming from all directions. At one point, she ran into me hard. I got harsh with her; more so than I normally would, but she was out of control far beyond what she had ever been since she was a pup. I think now the combination of being in a boat, where there was room for her to move around, and the first gunfire of the season, got her too worked up. I could not remember when she had last hunted out of a boat rather than the canoe, and strange situations sometimes cause dogs to behave out of character. She paid me back for being rough on her. When I sent her to retrieve the two birds I had knocked down, she did just fine going out and finding them. Then, instead of bringing them back to the boat, she brought them to a small island ten yards from the boat and put them there. She sat down near them and refused to come to me! She had never acted this way before, and I felt guilty about the chewing out I had given her.

The boys in the canoes each got a couple of birds, including Grant, who had never taken a duck before. Jill got to taste some feathers, though her performance would not be listed among her great ones. We hunted to the four o'clock close of shooting hours, and then I rowed the boat downstream and left it hidden in the brush alongside a rice-choked pool I wanted to hunt in the morning. Derek and Matt brought the gear to shore and then came downstream again to pick me up. With that, we were done for the day.

The second day of the duck season is almost as exciting as opening day. It is the first day (in Minnesota) you can hunt at sunrise. The noon opener sort of drives me nuts, as I hate waiting all morning for the opening bell. I have waited all year and it's something akin to making your kids wait until noon on Christmas day to open their presents. However, it does give opening weekend some added appeal. That second morning, as I said, is like a second opening day. Derek and I would be the only hunters that Sunday, and we were up hours before the sun. We had breakfast and drove back to Wawina, then drove the ATVs in to where our canoe was hidden. We paddled down to the pool where the boat was tucked into some thick rice and flooded willows. A couple of dozen duck decoys and six goose decoys were tossed out, some in the open pool and others here and there among the scattered rice stalks that grew out of the shallows. We hid the canoe and camouflaged the boat, which was to be our blind.

It was overcast and cool, but not cold. A few raindrops started to fall as we drank that wonderful first cup of coffee and watched the brightening sky to the east. We heard mallards, teal and wood ducks, waking up. Soon the first birds began flying up and down the river. As the legal shooting hour approached, I told Derek the next duck in range would get a salute. It was a mallard, and it came down-river about twenty feet off the water and thirty yards out. He crumpled at my shot. Now there were more birds in the air. In short order, I had two more and had not missed a shot. Then a knot of green-winged buzzed us low and I was humbled.

As the light increased, the ducks began working to the decoys. Our spread included one of the new-fangled, spinning wing contraptions. We had regular chances and knocked down several birds, sending Jill out now and again to pick them up. At one point, I waded out to help her with a wood duck that came down in the willows on the edge of the pool. As I returned with the bird, Derek made a great shot on a group of ducks that buzzed into the spread. They turned out to be widgeon, which we seldom see on my river.

After an hour or so, the birds were not flying much. Derek took a canoe trip down-river to try to jump some birds. I had five already, so only needed one to finish my limit. I got my chance when I saw a lone mallard drake approaching at high altitude. He was coming from up-river, on my right. As he passed overhead, I turned my head and got ready to give him a call. I was turning my face to look up, expecting to see him passing high overhead, when I heard the whistling of wings right above me. He had seen the decoys and I am sure it was the roboduck that got his attention so quickly. He had the brakes on and did a quick turn, coming right in as they do in the videos. It was an easy shot and my sixth and final duck was down in the decoys.

Derek returned, still two birds short of his limit. I got into the back of the canoe and began paddling upstream with Derek in the front end and ready to shoot. Before long, we jumped a group of green-winged teal, and Derek splashed one that came down in thick, flooded willows. Jill found the bird for us and we continued. We jumped more green-winged and missed. Shortly after that, we rounded a bend and a pair of mallards jumped off the water directly right in front of us. The drake rose in the classic fashion, nearly straight up, with his right side towards us. I saw it all perfectly from over Derek's shoulder. I remember thinking the rising birds looked just like the ones on the Minnesota Waterfowl Association logo. Derek's first shot folded the drake about six feet off the water and we had our limit. For a duck hunt on my river, this was extraordinary. I have killed a limit there on occasion, but only one other time did two of us fill out, and that was with five bird limits. We had twelve birds and a nice mix of mallards, wood ducks, two kinds of teal and the widgeon. I was pleased most by the fact that Derek got to have a real successful duck hunt, his first-ever limit of waterfowl.

We paddled back to the boat, picked up the decoys, and headed home. We got some nice photos of our two days worth of ducks. I had the next week off and hunted ducks all but two of the next seven days. The local birds seemed to clear out early. After the first weekend, I had sub-par hunting as far as the number of birds I took home. As always, I enjoyed my hours on the river. Other than the successful shoot that first Sunday, I had only one very good day of duck shooting in Minnesota that season. My next good shoots would come far to the south and much later in the coming winter.

Rats in the Rice

Since I was a lad, I have been in awe of trappers. Tales of the mountain men and the great hardships they endured in quest of beaver pelts were probably what piqued my initial interest. Later, many of the books I read involved trappers. I subscribed to Fur, Fish and Game magazine when I was about fourteen. My dad and some of his brothers had trapped for extra cash when they were young. A couple of Dad's friends and acquaintances were locally known as expert trappers and, to me, these men seemed like they had to have some supernatural abilities to be so admired by fellow woodsmen like Dad and his hunting peers.

I once visited one of these men and was treated to a tour of his trap preparation area. Behind his country home, there was a huge kettle. Here he boiled and waxed his traps over a wood fire. Nearby was a lean-to, where the traps were hung by their chain and ring, along with the steel drags that would tangle in the brush and hold the animal. He was a coyote trapper and a successful one. Of all the animals in Upper Michigan, coyotes were the toughest to trap. Successful coyote trappers were the best of the best. He had one of the little wolves there that day that he had just caught. He showed me that it was missing one foot from a previous encounter with a trap. It was healed over and it appeared from the way the scar tissue was formed, thick and worn, that the animal had been able to use the limb in spite of the fact that much of the foot was gone.

I don't know why I never attempted to trap back then. I suppose I thought I could never acquire that supernatural skill. I was content to daydream about one day living in a remote cabin with my dogs, living off the land and making my cash by trapping.

When my sons were young boys, I did give trapping a whirl one season. I wanted to try it with my kids, so we might have some fun together and perhaps learn a little about nature. When it actually came time to trap, the boys were busy with other things and I was, for the most part, on my own. I quickly gained even more respect for the trapper than what I had before. In my opinion, the best trappers are, without doubt, the most skilled practitioners of woodcraft. That is an opinion I have held for a long while. What I learned that first year, when I tried it myself, was how hard they have to work. Lugging a load of traps, an axe and the other miscellaneous items you need when you set out the trap-line, through beaver-flooded or logged areas, or even in reasonably open woods, will wear anyone out. My little trap-line consisted of only a few dozen sets for mink, muskrat, raccoon and fox. I only trapped for a week or two, and I am ashamed to tell you how poorly I did. My take was a single weasel. The traps were hung in the garage after that less than auspicious rookie year, and there they stayed until 1999.

As mentioned earlier, we have done much work on our property to create ponds and marshes for waterfowl and other wildlife. In addition to the pond construction, we have planted aquatic vegetation that is beneficial to these critters. This included several attempts to establish wild rice. The initial planting took place in the pool we call Bear Country Pond. It has an inlet and an outlet. Water flows through it from spring until about July, in normal years. When the fall rains come, the stream flows again. Rice needs some water exchange to grow and survive, so this pond seemed like the best place on the property for rice. The crop germinated beautifully. Soon, long rice stalks reached out of the clear water and into the sky. Rice kernels began to form, and things were looking great. Then the muskrats found it.

We had always had muskrats in the ponds. If you build it, they will come. I had enjoyed watching them from my deer stands, when I walked the banks of the ponds, or sat there to videotape the critters. They actually can help you with your wetland management by creating open areas in the marsh vegetation through their feeding. Ducks prefer wetlands that are fifty percent open water and fifty percent water with emergent vegetation. The pond we call Big Pond has an ash swamp just up the drainage from it, and here the muskrats had fed on the emergent plants for several years, creating those open water areas the ducks enjoyed. That first year we planted rice, as the shallower areas of the ponds dried up during the driest part of summer, the muskrats moved in to feed in the shallow water where the rice was growing. In a matter of days, every wild rice stalk had been nipped off at the water line before it could finish growing and drop its precious seed. A second attempt in the same pond a couple of years later ended exactly the same way.

The area I had planted in these first two attempts was very small, only an eighth of an acre or so. It was the only area in the

ponds that looked suitable for rice. However, in 1999, I had the excavator and bulldozer in action again. We created another acre or so of shallow water that had a little flow going through it most of the year. I seeded all of this to wild rice, and reseeded the pond where my first attempts had failed. This time, I decided to protect it.

I dug into my library, which has a book, or two, or five, on about everything outdoorsy. I found my two how-to books on trapping. I bought more traps. The kids got me one of those nifty, woven-wood trapper baskets and I bought some lure. I was in business.

During the summer I had cut some eight-foot long logs and split them in half. I put them along the edges of the open water, with one end up on shore or a hummock, and the other end reaching out into the water. Each formed a ramp from the water to the shore. Ducks and muskrats both like these "loafing sites" so they are ideal places for traps set up as drowning sets. I drove a nail into the submerged end of each log so I could wire the trap ring there. I waited for the opening of the trapping season and the weeklong vacation I had scheduled.

The Minnesota trapping rules allow you to set traps on opening day only after mid-morning. I had bundles of traps hung in trees by each of the ponds several days before the season opened. I had cut stakes for anchoring traps that would be set in locations other than the loafing log sets. I did a brief duck hunt on the opening day of the trapping season and began setting traps within minutes after the legal start time. I worked in waders and from my canoe, setting No.1 and No.1 1/2 long spring traps. I used No. 1 1/2 jump traps on the logs and on feeding platforms the "rats" make with the leftover stalks of cattails and other plants. I had some No.110 Conibears and some No.120's as well. These were set along the little highways made by the little busybodies through the cattails and rice. For someone who is new to this, making a "set" takes a bit of time, and I only got about two dozen sets out that first day. This is setting traps thickly, but I was not trapping for profit or even recreation. I was on a mission to save my valuable rice crop, which was doing beautifully. Evidently, the added area of rice was large enough that the existing muskrat population could not wipe it out as easily as they had the first two plantings. Hopefully, my trapping would keep the population down enough to ensure the survival of next year's crop.

When I made the last set of the day, I paddled the canoe back along the line of traps I had set, to beach it in the usual place. As I passed the second or third set I had made, I saw bubbles coming up from below the surface. I turned the canoe towards the trap site. As the feeding platform came alongside me, I saw the trap was gone. I fished for the wire and chain with the paddle and pulled up my first muskrat. Trapping was fun!

For the next week, I had a lot of fun. I duck hunted or bow hunted in the early mornings and checked my traps during the late morning or early afternoon. I put out more sets and sometimes I carried along my shotgun, managing to get some grouse and some ducks as I tended the traps. In the evenings, I would bow hunt. It was the good life. One evening I sat a stand for deer where I could see the slough, including a view of several of the muskrat sets. As the sun began to set, I saw a rat come out for his evening feeding. He cruised along, his tail doing the characteristic wiggle that propelled him cleanly through the water, the V of his wake disturbing the still surface. As he drew even with one of the loafing logs where I had a trap set, he turned in towards it. I could not quite see the area where the trap was set because of some weeds that obscured my view. I saw the rat get to the submerged end of the log and begin walking up. Just as he disappeared from view behind the weeds, I heard the snap of the trap and a splash. The muskrat rocketed a foot or so in the air, did a back flip and hit the water, immediately diving under with a kick of his back feet. The trap had been set too deep or too shallow. Something didn't work the way I had planned. One of those expert trappers will probably tell me exactly what happened. At any rate, the trap closed with no part of a rat caught in its jaws. Perhaps thirty seconds later, the rat appeared further down the pond and continued along on his evening journey.

I caught about fifteen muskrats that week. I caught five the first night and fewer each night as the week went on. Almost half of them were caught in an area no larger than a thirty-foot circle, three of them in the same set. I caught one muskrat foot as well. The animal did the famous (among trappers) twisting-off-the-foot trick to make his escape, leaving me with a severed foot as a souvenir. These numbers are not going to impress any real trappers, but I was happy.

I have trapped two years since 1999, catching fewer muskrats than I did that first year. I also caught three mink and was pleased about that. My wild rice is doing beautifully and hopefully, in another year, there will be four or five acres of it growing on the place, for a new wetland will be completed in the summer of 2002. Perhaps I will forego trapping this fall if I don't see too many of the little demons around during the spring and summer.

Muskrat are subject to population irruption. When one of these population explosions happens they can denude their ponds of all emergent vegetation. The population will eventually crash, and cattails and other types of plants will make a comeback, but I am not sure my rice crop would be resilient enough to do so. If I see such a thing happening, I will need to do some trapping. Otherwise, I might just leave the rats alone and hope they munch cattails and create openings for the ducks, instead of picking on the rice. If that is the case, I will not bother them. However, it's nice now, when I talk with other outdoorsmen, to be able to tell folks, "Yeah… I used to do some trappin'."

November

Most years, the northern Minnesota winter appears, and stays, during the month of November. Usually, by the second weekend of our deer season, say November 10 or so, the ground is snow covered and will stay that way until spring. By month's end, we have usually had our first below zero temperatures and the woods and marshes become quiet under nature's grip. The streams and lakes are frozen and the migratory birds long gone. Other wildlife has gone to ground or down into the mud to sleep the winter away. Early winter is pretty, but I miss the wildlife that leave each fall, or that become inactive during winter. As the years go by, I dislike winter more and more because of the cold, snow and inactivity. In recent years, the duck season in Minnesota has extended into November but, except for the large bodies of water, the lakes and streams are locked in ice, effectively ending my duck season. Grouse, too, can be hunted and one can do quite well. Before I had a dog, I used the snow to my advantage, looking for grouse tracks to key on the areas the birds were using. Often, grouse covey up for the winter. For the first time, since the family broods dispersed in early fall, there may be an opportunity to get into a big covey. Swamps that are normally too wet for walking are frozen over and the birds seem to like these areas. However, in 2001 the grouse were few and far between. Thankfully, there is deer season.

November Reunion

During the first years of my hunting experience, the rifle deer season was the most anticipated time of the entire year. It was a big event in my hometown, throughout the area, and among my male family members. I killed my first deer in 1968 when I was fifteen years old. After that, although I hunted every year save one, I did not kill another until 1977. That one was taken with bow and arrow. I then did very well with bow hunting, but shot only one other deer with a rifle until 1990 or so. Then, I managed to take three nice bucks in three years with firearms. All of these were shot with my dad's old Model 99, 300 Savage and with open sights. The gun was obviously lucky.

Many people enjoy the social aspects and camaraderie of hunting as much as, or more than, the actual hunting. I suppose I am cut from different cloth and, for the most part, I enjoy the hunt much more than the social aspects. I hunt by myself far more often than I do in the company of others. However, the rifle deer season is the one type of hunting, and the one time of the hunting season, when I enjoy the hoopla and the company of other hunters as much as I do the hunting. The 2001 Minnesota season kicked off a very special year of firearms deer hunting for me.

Until recently, I had a lot of deer-hunting territory almost to myself right near my home. Now, much of that territory was either not available to me, or crowded with other hunters. Because of this, our firearm season is spent mostly on the seventy-seven acres I own. We have not had great success there in taking deer, except for one year when we took three bucks from our place, two of them the first morning. Usually it was my son, Danny, a few of his friends, and me. Occasionally other friends would join us for a day or weekend. The 2001 Minnesota firearm season was special for two reasons. Those two reasons were my son, Ben, and my cousin, Doug. Ben is not very keen on hunting and had not hunted for several years, but decided to join us for the rifle season. He did so to spend some time with his dad and brother, and I am happy he did. I had always dreamed my sons and daughter would come home to hunt the firearms season with me, and for the first time in years, that dream came true. My daughter, Tara, has joined me for deer hunting on and off since she was old enough to go. Doug had also gotten away from hunting, for perhaps thirty-five years or so. For whatever reason, he decided to buy a rifle and try it again. When I heard this I immediately invited him to join us, and he accepted.

The season was warmer than usual, and the deer that had been running all over the property during the summer and early fall seemed to disappear. Just west of our land is a large field that had a good crop of lush clover growing in it, and just west of that, there is about sixty acres of lowland brush that is an ideal bedding ground for deer. All fall, a large group of does and fawns had been feeding on the clover and bedding in that brush. I suspect as these does began coming into heat, the bucks in my woods started to spend more and more time with them. Because of this, they were not on their usual grounds, where I had watched them during the summer and early fall. At any rate, we saw few deer, and none we could say for sure were bucks. One evening, Ben was on stand near the backfield and had a deer walk into view and pass by at a distance, then move onto the neighbor's property. Immediately there was a shot. The path this deer had taken was the same we had seen being used by a spike buck during the archery season so I suspect it was that same spike buck, though we never learned this for sure.

In the evenings, after the hunt, others who were hunting in the area joined us at my home. There were hunters from my

father-in-law's party and from another neighborhood deer camp. There was a lot of good company and laughter in the house, and plenty of food. My three-year old grandson, Ben's little boy, Connor, was with us too. I found myself often quitting my hunts early to spend some time playing with him back at the house. Each time I came in, he would look up and say, "Soot a dee-yer?" I got a little tired of saying no, but not of his inquiries.

We hunted two weekends. We sat the stands and we made drives. We never fired a shot. One afternoon, while making a drive, I found a dead doe that had been gut shot and lost. It was too far gone to be used. Doug put in a fair bit of stand time, and though he had no chances at a buck, he says he will be back. We have plans to set up some stands together in the spring. I told him he could pick a spot for himself. It is always good to have people invest time in the off-season preparations. It adds to the whole allure of the hunt.

For the story of a successful Minnesota deer hunt in November, I have to turn to things I have experienced and recorded years ago. When I say successful, I am speaking in terms of the harvest only. The satisfaction of being with old friends and family made November 2001 a great rifle season.

November 1990

My son Danny had a Friday off from school towards the end of the season, so I decided to take a day off work to hunt with him. My father-in-law planned to join us that morning, but as we were finishing breakfast, he called and begged off. Seems he had also promised his Mrs. to take her on a trip to Michigan and she would not let him out of it. So it was just Danno and I, which is really about my favorite hunting group anyway.

The wind direction and snow conditions were perfect for trying a little maneuver I had wanted to do for a while. Starting at my in-laws house, we would take turns making little pushes to each other, heading east down the long "Baumo's camp" ridge that stretched like a peninsula into the Toivola swamp. The man on the move would just kind of poke along hoping for a shot, but also be moving deer around. We hoped those deer would go past the stander. Fresh, fluffy snow coming down assured us we would be able to read sign easily as to age, this in turn letting as know when we moved deer. In that case, the mobile hunter would try to track the critter and move it to the partner, or again get a crack at it himself. We took the field just at first light, later than normal but only because of the operation we were doing.

Danny took stand first and I began by walking through Marty's back yard and through some cuttings on my way to him. This simple little drive has been very productive for us, but this time nothing was there to move. I then circled around and took a stand on the logging road while Danny pushed a piece of high ground and through a spruce swamp. Again, we saw nothing, but Danny found some fresh sign. He then circled out to the east and I took my turn being the hound. Soon I cut fresh tracks. Several deer, including one with a big track and traveling alone, had moved to the east from the area Danny had just driven. I was quite sure the deer had gone through before my partner had gotten into his current position. When I came through to him, he confirmed he had seen the tracks on his way to this post. I had him move again in a half-circular route that took him southwards first, then east to a permanent stand at Baumo's camp. This had been a popular crossing and ambush spot for Marty's gang for years. I gave him fifteen minutes or so to get into position and began tracking this group of deer.

Our positions at the start of this were as follows. Picture the letter capital T.

The top of the T is the main ridge, running east and west. (Actually, the top of the T should be much longer then the vertical leg, but there ain't no letter like that so you just have to use your imagination.) Danny is at the left (east) end of the top of the T. I am at the very base, to the north. The vertical leg is a point of high ground jutting out into the huge bog. Right between us is a black spruce bog, the kind with the spongy hummocks of moss and Labrador tea, etc. The spruce swamp turns into open bog near where Danny is. There are a couple of little islands of high ground there, which deer often bed on. That is where I fig-ured these deer had gone. The eight-pointer I killed six days earlier had passed through this spruce bog on his way to his final bed. I started along the trail.

The shadowy world of the spruce was quiet and magical. Fresh snow on the boughs reflected what light there was and made it brighter than normal, but it was still much darker than the surrounding, more open woodland. Chickadees seem to love these thick conifer stands when it is snowing. They cheer it up. They "Dee dee'd" as I moved along the tracks, trying to pick out quiet spots to step while still watching ahead for signs of the deer. The entire group, including the big one, was on the same trail now. They started to bend to my left, so I swung wide in the hopes of cutting them off and getting them to go back south

towards Danny. I cut more tracks that were headed east. It now appeared I had a half-dozen deer in front of me. Hopefully, they were still between Danny and me. As I got to the little islands, I found two of them had gotten by me and headed north into the big bog. But neither was the big-footed one. I carefully moved down the islands towards my boy, trying to move slowly and to sort of quarter back and forth to move the deer in front of me.

Soon I spotted Danny in the stand a hundred yards away. There was only one small bump of high ground left to cross, and it was only about twenty by forty feet. As I got within twenty-five yards of it, I heard an explosion of breaking brush and caught the blur of movement ahead. It was heading north and would pass by to the east of me, going away from Danny. I moved quickly to a small lane in the brush that had been cleared years before. It ran right between where Danny and I were. The lane was narrow and brushy, but it was my only hope and the deer was headed towards it. I brought up my gun, Dad's old model 99 Savage. I was shooting it with the original peep sights it had come with and I pointed it to where I guessed the deer was going to cross. I picked the right spot, but the brush on either side of the opening was so thick I had no warning before he suddenly launched himself across the lane. It was over much quicker than it takes to tell it. I was left in the quiet of the swamp, snowflakes slowly floating down, my gun still shouldered and pointed towards the now empty shooting lane.

It was a buck. I never saw the horns but I knew it was a buck. It was big, blocky and dark with a neck thick and swollen with the rut. There had been no huge leaps and no waving flag of a tail, just the low flat beeline like a bullet train through the brush and into the big bog to the north. It was a buck all right. And he had just given us the slip.

I moved in to where he had been bedded, and it appeared he was probably laying down there when Danny got in the stand. It was also obvious why he went north instead of east or south where Danny could have had a crack at him. As I knelt in the bed, I could see Danny plain as day. Mr. Buck had watched him climb into the stand. Well, it was time to consult my partner. I walked over to him and we sat down on a log to eat some lunch and discuss our next move.

Danny would stay at this stand. I would track the buck. If the buck turned east, there was a good chance I could move it by Danny. If it turned west, I would fire a shot to signal Danny to move to a stand location in that area. The day was still young and we had a good buck close to us. Tracking conditions were ideal and the bog was just frozen enough that, with caution, I could walk through it without getting wet. At least I hoped so.

When I began to track him, I found the buck had gone only a short distance on the jump, and then slowed to a trot. He cut into an old winter logging road that was free of brush and followed it for a bit. Soon he had slowed to a walk.

The bog here is covered with a varying degree of brush, alder and willow, stunted by the wet and acidic conditions. An occasional spruce or birch grew out of dryer spots and the wetter spots actually had cattails growing out of them. Leatherleaf and Labrador tea dominate the plant community. In spots, you could see 150 yards. Hummocks provided the best chance for not getting my feet wet. In places, the heavily used deer paths were frozen. They looked like inviting sidewalks. I always had to step on ice that had grass or sticks in it for reinforcement, or the ice would give way. There was some deep water out there, so caution was called for. Not that I would drown or even get hypothermia, but it would sure put the kibosh to the morning hunt if I got wet to the waist.

I picked my way slowly, watching up ahead, and watching my footing. The buck was walking now. Before long he began meandering, showing he was slowing. Relaxing or watching his back trail? Either way, it looked like there was a good chance I would catch up to him.

Every forty or fifty steps I would get up on one of the higher hummocks to get a better look around. We were in an open part of the bog now and my pulse was quickening. Suddenly a flash of white! I saw that blocky physique broadside as it walked into a screen of brush, the tail flared wide but held low. It had flickered out to a horizontal position just for a second and that was what caught my eye. He was about seventy yards out, screened by brush and I was atop a hummock with my only possible shot being from an offhand position. For a marginal marksman like me, it was hardly an easy opportunity, but ya takes whatcha get when you hunt deer, and I took it.

At the shot, the deer disappeared. I saw nothing after the recoil pulled my eyes off the deer. I levered in a fresh round and watched for movement. Nothing. I approached the area where he had been standing cautiously. There! Tracks leading away. I followed and noticed that it was obvious the deer was not moving with a normal gait. A few more yards and I spotted a small trickle of blood on the snow. I was into it now, a wounded buck way out in the big bog. I made a quick circle of the area to see if there were any other tracks to indicate another deer had paired up with this guy. I would have to shoot fast if I caught up to the wounded animal and I wanted to be sure he wasn't now traveling with a doe. I saw no other tracks, so I took the blood trail. Suddenly, I remembered Danny would be moving west if he heard a single shot. I fired another just for a signal, and then proceeded with my tracking.

I had only proceeded a hundred yards or so, and with the deer moving along pretty well I wasn't really expecting to see it for a bit yet. Suddenly though, there he was only thirty yards away! It was the first good look I had at the rack and it was mighty impressive for a so-so deer hunter like muhself. It was wide, dark and thick. The tips of the tines didn't curve in; they spread out wider, giving the impression the rack was opening up to catch something that was falling from the sky. He was a nice mature buck and he was hurt. He took off, but not with the typical motion of an escaping deer, rather with kind of a bouncing stride like the one a moose has. He was in an opening in the brush and when I had entered that opening, he spotted me and took off as best he could. He was moving straight away and I held the sights on the center of his hind end. I did not want to shoot him in the rear if I didn't have to, but he was wounded and he was heading north into a swamp that stretched for a dozen miles or more with no houses, roads or trails. If he didn't turn before he got to the edge of the opening, I would shoot him up the vent. I didn't have to. He turned slightly to his left, as he ran, not running very well due to the wound. I remember it so clearly. It was as if it was happening in slow motion. I have heard many people describe the slow motion thing, which I think must have something to do with being in an adrenaline "enriched" state. It sounds kind of grisly when I tell it, but man it was something. When he turned, the gun was already up and waiting. When I shot, hair exploded from just in front of the hindquarter where the slug struck and entered. It also flew from the neck where it exited. I even remember the plumes of hair being different color, the exit plume being the white hair from the throat patch. The shot and impact turned him to his right, almost broadside to me now, but still moving. The Savage is a sweet handling weapon and I was on him again and gave him another. Another plume of hair erupted into the air and the bucks hind legs wilted. His front hooves were still under him, but he was done for and he never tried to pull himself away with his front legs.

He would have died soon, but I didn't like the look in his eyes as his life ebbed away, so I ended it instead in an instant.

Again the swamp was silent and the only movement was the sifting downward of the snowflakes. I looked at this monster lying on his belly and counted the ten points on the rack. Gosh, he was a beauty. His face was sprinkled with gray-white hair and the top of his head was black, unusually black. His rack was dark and heavy. The rut-swollen neck was huge. He was absolutely beautiful. I tracked down the bugger in the big swamp and I got him. Man it was good. If you do not hunt, you may now be shaking your head wondering what kind of sick man I am. If you are a real hunter, you are now thinking how right I am about how good it feels.

The buck turned out to weigh 180 pounds. Not a giant, but a good mature buck and the best I had ever killed. One of the neatest things about this hunt was how excited Danny was when he joined me to gut the deer. He seemed as excited as if he had killed the buck himself. It was very unselfish enthusiasm. We had a heck of a job getting this guy out of the bog. It was impossible to stay on top of the ice without breaking through when you were dragging the deer. Danny, his friend Brandon, and I pulled him out. It took from about 10:30 A.M. until 4:30 P.M., when we finally hooked him up to Marty's four-wheeler. We motored the last half-mile to load him on our vehicle. We were three whipped puppies by the time we got him hung in the garage and headed to my in-law's restaurant in Floodwood for supper. I ached from head to toe, wanted sleep real bad, and grinned like an idiot for about three days.

Tracking down a buck like this is not an easy task. Why he didn't just bolt when I caught up to him is a mystery. His flared white tail told me he was alarmed and that's what caught my eye just before I shot. Then he stopped in the brush to look at me. That is not characteristic of a mature whitetail buck. I theorize this buck had escaped into the bog many times and had never ever been followed there before I took his trail into that mess on that snowy day. When he heard me on his trail, he probably thought I was one of the other deer, so rather than high tail it, he just cautiously stepped into cover to assess the situation. We will never know for sure, but persistence paid off for me by sticking to the trail until he made a mistake.

I have a nice photo of the buck and me, taken while we took a breather from dragging him. I have an enlargement of it on the wall in my den and another in my hunting photo album. The buck is slung over one of the hummocks and that lovely white face with the black crown is obvious. You can see the brushy bog in the background and Dad's old 300 is resting on the buck's side. I am holding up the rack and I look tired. You can see a rip in the knee of my hunting pants and the collar of my coat is loose and you can see I have no shirt on underneath. That was because I was sweating so hard from dragging the beast. In the album, I put a quote from Robert Ruark's classic book The Old Man and The Boy. He wrote it when he tells about his first buck. Although the circumstances are not exactly the same as my swamp buck experience, the emotions are identical. It goes like this.

"He was beautiful gold on his top and dazzling white on his underneath and his little black hoofs were clean. The circular tufts of hair on his legs, where the scent glands are, were bright russet and stiff and spiky. His horns were as clean as if they had been scrubbed with a wire brush, gnarled and evenly forked and the color of the planking on a good boat that's just been holy-stoned to where the decks sparkle. This was my buck. Nobody else had shot him. Nobody else had seen him but me. Nobody had advised or helped. This monster was mine."

Back to Black River

For years I had thought, and talked of, returning to Upper Michigan to hunt again on the grounds where I first took up the sport. The old camp my dad built in the late 1940s—the place that was like Shangri La to me as a boy—was now owned by my cousins, and still in use. My cousins, Chas and Rod, had told me many times to come to hunt with them there. In 2000, I tried to arrange things at the last minute to go there for a hunt, but things at the office got in the way and I wasn't able to go. However, my son, Danny, and I had begun planning early in 2001 that we would hunt in Michigan that November. The Michigan season always opens on November 15, which fell in mid-week that year. I scheduled time off beginning the 14th through the long Thanksgiving weekend. I planned to be in Michigan for opening day and to return home the day before Thanksgiving to be with family, here in Minnesota. Danny would join up with us at the camp on Friday, November 16. Our plan was to hunt from the camp with Chas and his crew for the first several days, then join Uncle Chuck Prusi at his camp for a couple of days. Uncle Chuck is the last surviving brother of my dad and had spent time and effort on me when I was a lad. I wanted to spend some time with him, and he was excited to have us. He was in his mid-seventies, and still an avid deer hunter. He spent nearly the entire season at his camp each year.

I had hunted six or seven seasons in Michigan when I was a young man. Only one of those November 15 openers had been

snow free. However, when I got to Black River on the day before the season in 2001, the ground was bare and the temperature balmy. I did not mind. I drove straight to the camp and it felt good to be driving there for a hunt. The camp neighborhood hasn't changed much. A large percentage of the scattered homes there are those of relatives. My mother grew up less than a half-mile from the camp, on the homestead my grandfather carved out of that rugged and rocky forest. When I see the rocks and hills of that area, I realize what a tough man he had to have been to farm this country.

My dad and two of his brothers had married girls from this neighborhood. They obviously saw its potential for hunting four-legged deer as well. Uncle Biff moved here after marrying one of the local girls. Dad and Uncle Bill began to hunt the area as well, traveling from their homes a half-hour away. All nine brothers would end up hunting this area for at least part of their hunting careers. Four of the brothers had a camp behind Biff's house, just a couple of miles from ours. Uncle Walfred had a camp not far away, and Uncle Chuck eventually built one about fifteen miles away. Dad's sister, Irene, married a local boy, Jake Hintsala. Uncle Jake also has a camp, where his sons and grandsons hunt every year. One might say that Black River is the historic hunting grounds of the Prusi clan.

When I pulled into the camp yard, Chas and my brother-in-law, Phil, were there. They were hanging bedding on tree limbs around the yard to air them out, and giving the place a general cleaning. I joined in and we got the place in fair shape. Phil and I went into town for supplies. We got back to camp at a reasonable hour. Hunting out of the camp, besides the three of us, would be Chas's sons, Josh and Jake; Danny, and Rod's son, Justin. I can't remember who showed up when, but by Friday night, we were all there.

It felt rather strange, but pleasant, to be spending deer season eve at the camp again. I recalled those evenings of thirty plus years before, when Dad and I had hauled our gear into the camp and got things set up for our stay. Uncle Charley, my mom's brother who lived just up the hill, would have the fuel oil space heater started for us and the camp was warm and cozy. The groceries were put away and the guns placed in a corner. Often, we would listen to our Negaunee Miner basketball team's game on the radio.

One year we found the camp overrun with mice. I searched around and found one mousetrap up in the rafters, but when I tested it, I found the trigger was bent and it would take more than a mouse to fire it. I rounded up a piece of conduit pipe about eight feet long, and I set the trap under the table, somehow rigging the pipe in a way that I could fire the trap by jiggling the pipe. I leaned the other end of the pipe on one of the bunk beds and lay there waiting for a mouse. The ball game was on and Dad sat quietly in the old rocker, listening to the game and occasionally giving me a grin or a comment on my elaborate plan. We sat there quietly. The only sound was the basketball game on the radio, and the volume was set low.

The mice were bold after having the camp to themselves, for who knows how many months. Soon they were scurrying about in plain sight. One found my peanut butter baited trap and began to nibble. I jiggled the pipe and the mouse was mine. Dad gave me a grin of approval and asked me if I was going to skin out my prize. As the evening went on, I caught two more the same way. I don't remember how the Miner basketball team did, but eventually we turned in. I lay there thinking of a trophy buck, listening to the surviving mice running amuck in our food supply and watching the flicker of the oil fire in the little window on the space heater door.

I fell asleep there that night in 2001 with these treasured memories floating through my mind.

Opening morning 2001 was warm and foggy. Our hunters divided into three groups. Phil and I would hunt just northeast of the camp, the area where "Walt's Spot," "Point Abby," "The Swamp Blind," and "Violators" are found. These are all the names of deer blinds; the first is named for my dad. Justin and Josh headed for "the 600" which is a 600-acre parcel owned by a logger who had granted permission for hunting to the group for several years. The others would go "behind George's." George was my uncle, who lived for years on the homestead where my mother was born and raised. It wasn't actually George's place anymore, but for us, that piece of woods will always be "behind George's."

I got to hunt Dad's old blind. The guys wanted me to go there and I was happy to oblige. Phil and I drove in on a logging road and parked the truck just off the right-of-way of a gas pipeline, not far from "Bill Rowe's Rock." Dad's spot was on a knob just down the gas-line. It was very warm and I carried my heavy coat in with me and wore no gloves. It was very odd to have heavy fog and dew in mid-November, and it was so very still. I walked about 250 yards or so to the knob and there was the blind, built of logs and covered with boughs. I sat down in the old metal chair inside the blind and arranged my gear. The gloves and coat were put aside for now, I wouldn't put them on until I started to get cool.

I levered open the action on Dad's old 300 and pushed the gleaming brass cartridges down into the rotary magazine. Dad had purchased the gun new, just before U.S. factories switched over to military weapons production for World War II. He had carried it for over thirty deer seasons and killed many deer with it, including some beautiful bucks. I inherited the gun and had not used it much at all until about 1990, when I decided to start using it as my primary deer-hunting weapon. That first year, I killed two nice bucks with it and two years later, another. Now, both the gun and I were having a sort of homecoming. To my left and across the gas-line right-of-way was where Dad—with this rifle—had killed his last buck, an eight-pointer, in 1970. Dad died the following May. The first season after his death, I had cried myself to sleep that first night in camp. I hunted two more seasons there without him and then moved to Minnesota. This was my first time back to hunt since. I had wondered if I would feel sadness. I felt emotion, but not sadness. Neither was it joy. It was good to be here. Maybe what I felt was relief that I was not sad. At any rate, I felt good.

I sat in the blind until close to noon. I didn't need to put on the coat until eleven or so. It was foggy, still, and warm. I heard turkeys and goats from a nearby farm and not too many shots. A couple of ducks flew over, mergansers I think. When I left the stand, I walked towards "Point Abby," which was built on or near the day when Chas's first and only daughter, Abby, was born. I spotted Phil there sound asleep on the ground. I walked up and stood right over him until he woke up. We had a chuckle and visited a bit. Then I walked around until it was time to take evening watch. I finished the first day without seeing a deer.

I hunted three very full days in the area surrounding Dad's old blind. The weather was more like early autumn or even late summer. The deer were not moving around much and I never saw so much as a tail. Still, I enjoyed myself, tramping over the old hunting grounds. We left the camp in the darkness each morning and drove in close to the hunting spot. We remained outdoors until dark, and then returned to the camp. Danny arrived on Friday and hunted with Phil and me in the same area. Some of the group saw deer but nobody got a chance at a buck. Evenings were spent around the camp or visiting at Chas's house. His grandsons were home, and just as I had a tough time staying away from my grandson while he was at my place during the Minnesota season, Chas seemed anxious to be with his little guys in the evenings. We had wonderful visits and plenty of laughs.

Of course, besides hunting, a deer camp has a lot of tomfoolery going on at any one time. There is a lot of razzing going on at Walt's camp, whenever two or more are gathered there. It was that way when I hunted there as a teenager and nothing much has changed. If you mess up, be it on a shot at a deer or buying the wrong kind of pancake mix, you are going to hear about it daily for the rest of the season. Most likely, you will hear about it occasionally for the rest of your life. In fact, you don't really have to mess up. All it takes is for someone to perceive that you messed up and tell someone about it. This is not the criminal justice system where you are innocent until proven guilty. It's a dog-eat-dog competition and if you can get the crew hounding one of the other guys, there is at least a chance they will stay off your own back. I still get it from some of these guys on things I did over thirty years ago.

In our family, there is a belief, or legend, or maybe it is a hope, that there is some royal blood in our lineage. At the camp, all the hunters were Prusi men, except for Phil, who married into the clan. We refer to such folk as "outlaws" because it sounds so much better to us than in-law. At any rate, one day there was a miscom-munication involving the fetching of a cooler full of food. I don't remember the exact details, but what Phil thought he was sup-posed to do with this cooler did not match what everyone else thought he was supposed to do. After he was chastised (verbally, but less than gently) by one or more hunters, he made the mistake of trying to explain his actions. Chas listened politely to his protest, then turned to me shaking his head and said, very solemn-ly, "Boy, you can sure tell he don't have the blood," referring to Phil's lack of royal lineage. Phil was promptly given the name "the Commoner" for the remaining day or two of the hunt.

It also seems to be standard operating procedure to belittle another hunter's buck. There is an unwritten and unspoken code of conduct in this. In reality, if someone gets a deer they them-selves are happy with, I think everyone in the group feels good. However, you cannot tell the shooter that. When the successful hunter is present in a group, it is not considered bad form to demean the quality of his trophy. Nobody would say such a thing behind his back or to his face one-on-one. There would be no point. If someone is lucky enough to shoot a real good buck, one with unassailable trophy quality, the hunter himself will be the butt of the jabs. He will have gotten the buck through luck or the hard work of someone else, and will be somehow undeserving. We had a tough time with this routine during my comeback year because nobody shot anything during the camp week. However, near the end of the season, Chas did close his eyes and lob a shell that somehow fatally wounded a tiny buck.

I managed to find a documented example of the "trophy/hunter-skills trashing" in the camp logbook. It was writ-ten by Chas to describe the buck that Rod took in 2000. Rod had hunted for several days with no success. The money was still in the "buck pool" as nobody had scored. On his last day in camp, Rod cleaned up and packed his gear. He then decided to walk to the top of the hill behind the camp and sit for a little while, watching a bait pile the fellows had kept there all season. Apparently, Phil was recovering from the rigors of the past several days, asleep inside the camp. Rod was only on stand for a little while when a small buck came in and Rod shot it. It was a great "last minute of the hunt" success story. The log entries are classic. Here is Rod's:

Nov. 19, 2000
As you can see, I was able to send a message to the local deer.
If you investigate the kill site, you will see that he ran about 150 yards.
I was able to drive close to the deer and dragged him with my truck part of the way. You may notice that I attempted to climb the hill in a couple of places. However, due to the massive weight of this deer even my trusty Dakota could not make the climb.
With superhuman strength, I was able to hoist him into the back of the truck and drive him to the camp. Anyone who is willing to take the grizzled old fella can have him.
Rod
P.S. Phil slept through the whole thing.
P.P.S. I guess the buck pool money is mine.

Chas then followed up with his own commentary. You will observe there is a bit of difference in the political leanings of the two brothers as well.

5th Day -- Hunters - Phil, Chas, Justin, Joe
Butchers - Rod (of let 'em go, let 'em grow fame)
Sightings - Phil - 0, Chas - 7, Justin - 0, Joe - 0, Rod - In barnyard - 1 white-tail fetus pet spikie minnow slaughtered over pile of corn at 60 yards with mammoth 270 cal. rifle scoped with Leupold Vari-X III. Used 9 power to stretch spikes just to win $5.00 buck pool in typical Bush - Republican Style - "Read My Lips."

You can see why hunting at Walt's camp is an experience one does not forget.

The fourth morning, I slept in when the others left for morning watch. Sleeping in is a relative term of course. I was up a little after the sun. I washed dishes, organized my gear and enjoyed some quiet time in the camp I loved so much as a boy. I drove over to Uncle Biff's camp and visited for a while with five of my cousins there. For all but one of them, deer season is more of a social event than a time of serious efforts to fill the freezer. In fact, they admitted, with just a little embarrassment, that on opening day, the weather had been so nice they all decided to go golfing rather than hunt. While they were there, they discovered the local television station news was doing some filming at the course. I don't know the nature of the story that was being shot. The fact that people would golf when they could be deer hunting, especially in Upper Michigan, is something I certainly found newsworthy. The evening news shows are full of such tragedies. In deference to my cousins, who successfully escaped being caught in that act on film, I will mention no names.

It was great to see these guys. The old camp building is gone now, replaced by a nice, new building. Still, my nostalgia got the best of me as I drove away. I remembered my last visit here during hunting season, the year after I lost my dad. The old building was much more along the lines of the classic deer shack and, of course, when I was there thirty years ago, the uncles were still a part of the picture.

The new generation of hunters that use Biff's camp have placed a nice memorial to the four original members. Four trees, one for each brother, were planted on the edge of the camp yard. A fence around each protects them from wildlife damage. I suppose the deer might seek their revenge by browsing the limbs or perhaps a buck would rub his antlers on the trunks and girdle the bark off them. So, the memorial trees are protected. I can't think of a nicer tribute to Biff, George, Alex and Leo Prusi.

Back at the camp, the crew was gathered for a midday rest and meal. Danny and I loaded our gear and said goodbye. It had been a good trip, and a wonderful hunt. Neither Danny nor I had seen a deer. It would have been a better story had Danny or I killed a buck from Dad's old blind, and I think everyone was wishing for that. I know I was. Yet, we were far from disappointed and we still had some hunting to do.

As mentioned, Uncle Chuck Prusi is in his seventies, and the last survivor of the nine Prusi brothers. When I visited him last in the summer of 2000, he knew how many days there were until deer season. Retired, he spends the entire deer season at his camp except for a trip in on Thanksgiving Day to be with his family.

When I was a boy, Chuck took an interest in me and made time for me. He brought me things that I thought I needed and he took me hunting when my dad could not. He was, and still is, very good to me. My dad was ten years older than Chuck and had taken him hunting when he was young, as did some of the other older brothers. In the summer of 2000, Chuck had told me some stories of those hunts and of his relationship with my dad.

One of the nicest stories was about when he was still living at the family farm with his folks. Dad and Uncle Bill were both married and living away. When they came to visit at the farm, they would have Chuck dig potatoes from the garden for them. In the fall of that year, Dad and Bill presented Chuck with a brand new, single-shot, Remington .22, putting him on top of the world.

I was anxious to spend time with him and to have my son and my uncle get to know each other. Several family members had told me Chuck's health had declined since I had seen him last. When I talked with him about our hunt, I pressed him a little to make sure he was not just planning on hunting because I was going to be there. He assured me he would be at his camp, and hunting, whether anyone came to join him or not.

We had a little trouble finding the camp. The camp roads in upper Michigan are like mazes—narrow, winding, and with plenty of intersections. Nevertheless, we eventually found the place and said hello to Uncle Chuck, his grandson, Andy, Andy's friend, Chris, and Chris's dad, Terry. Another fellow named Fred was there too, but was leaving camp that afternoon. Andy and Chris are twelve and this year, could hunt deer with bow and arrow for the first time. Each had taken a button buck, right in the camp yard. They had a bait pile set up between the camp and the outhouse and sat on a chair on the camp roof to watch it! Those two deer were the only ones anyone had taken out of the camp thus far.

We visited a while and then took a ride with Uncle Chuck so he could show us some watching spots he had picked for us. He had aged a lot in the sixteen months since I had last seen him and moved very slowly. He walked us part way into the area we were to hunt and then returned to camp while we hunted the evening watch. After supper that night, the youngsters returned to civilization, leaving Danny, Chuck, Terry and me.

We spent three days with Uncle Chuck. Hunting was not very productive and I kept my record clean by not seeing a single deer. Danny got a look at one or two does, and Terry shot a doe on the bait pile by the outhouse one afternoon as he left the camp for evening watch. Chuck, Danny and I were sitting inside as Terry left, and a few seconds later we heard him shoot, right outside the camp. We all looked at each other, said hardly anything and waited. Terry walked in, laughing, and saying he had one down in the yard. We walked outside as Terry told us how he came out and saw the deer as he got ready to leave for his evening hunt. It was looking right at him. He slowly walked to his truck, which was between him and the deer. He got out his gun, loaded it and took a rest on the truck. The deer just kept staring at him and he shot it in the neck.

"It just kept staring at me!" Terry laughed.

Chuck put a very serious look on his face and said, "They shouldn't stare at a guy like that." This gave us all a good laugh.

We gutted the deer, a decent size doe, and hung her up on a tripod in the yard.

Chuck's grandson had built him a blind close to the camp, so his grandpa would not have to travel far to hunt. Each day, Chuck got out for morning and evening watch, slowly walking to his blind on the hill above the camp. One day, though, Danny and I were on our own hilltops and we saw another hunter moving along slowly below us. It turned out that it was Chuck. He evidently needed to get a little farther from the Camp at least once while we were there. It was obvious he was ailing. Like so many of his brothers, he has a bad heart. Medication is the only treatment for his particular problem. It obviously was not making him feel very healthy and it was hard to see him so feeble. Yet he still had his sense of humor and was quick with a wise crack like the one about the deer staring at Terry.

It was very bittersweet to be there. I will always be glad I got in another hunt with my uncle, but it was very difficult for me to see him in this condition. On the walls of the main living area in the camp are two beautiful mounts of eight-point bucks he had killed.

There was also a wonderful black and white photograph of him, framed and on the wall, with his first buck. It was a seventeen-pointer and he got it in Black River while hunting with my dad. He was in his late teens and he cuts a very handsome figure in the photo. He is young, strong and good-looking. His face wears the wide smile of a successful hunter. He is kneeling alongside the monster buck, holding his 30-30 in his right hand. In the background are Dad's car and the old camp they hunted out of before our camp was built. It was difficult for me to look at that picture and to remember the good times Chuck had shown me, and then look at him in the rocking chair. He was old and he was ill.

I have thought often of that evening, and thanked my lucky stars we got to spend some time together. It was reassuring to see his good nature and sense of humor were intact, even though he was very tired. This trip was not about shooting deer and it was not even about having fun. It was about doing something that was good for three generations of family. It was simply the right thing to do.

We left for home two days before Thanksgiving. Danny rode with me and we laughed and talked about the fun we had and about the importance of family. We talked about what a great guy Uncle Chuck was. We also talked about Danny's girlfriend, and it was the first time I heard from him just how much he cared about her. I knew he would be asking her to marry him. Another big step in his life's progression. Perhaps one reason men love to hunt together is they can relax. Only when they relax in such an environment can they share the things that need to be shared. This was a good trip. I never saw a deer and I even felt some sadness. Nevertheless, it was a very good trip.

I have no immediate plans to return for another hunt in Michigan. I may well hunt there again, but I have not set another Michigan hunt as one of my goals. It would be nice to hunt there with Rod, who couldn't be there in 2001. If Danny wants to begin a tradition of traveling there to hunt, I will likely join him. I cannot really explain the emotions I feel about hunting there. It was a homecoming, but I realize these are no longer "my stomping grounds." My friends and family made me feel more than welcome and their company is second to none. I guess I feel I accomplished a mission when I finally made it back to Black River and to Chuck's camp. If I return, I will enjoy it. If I do not, I will remember the hunt I made there in 2001.

As I grow older, the memories of my hunting trips have taken on a different flavor. While the memory of game taken is still an important part of this memory "library," other things now have a more prominent place. Things like a great retrieve the dog made or some unusual natural event. There are also those special recollections of being around the table at the camp again. Laughing and joking with my hunter cousins, some of them the third generation to call that camp their home during the deer season each year. Reflections on conversations about the serious issues in life and about men, now gone, who had hunted here. I will remember my son listening to stories about the grandfather he never met, told by Uncle Chuck, who had been taken under my dad's wing, and who had taken me under his own. The stories, for the most part, were those I had heard a dozen times or more. Nevertheless, I took great pleasure in hearing them told to my son, by my uncle. I will remember a hunter grown old and tired in body, but with the same sense of humor and the same desire to be "out the camp" during the deer season. That has never changed. Perhaps most of all, I will remember that day on the high hardwood ridge when I saw him moving so slowly through the valley below, pushing himself just a little more than he should have, to spend another morning on a favorite deer stand.

I should add that the buck Chas shot, late in the season, was not a "spikey minnow." Also, he killed it with a single shot at over 400 yards.

December

In December, we are likely to see our first long-lasting periods of bitter cold. While we may rarely get through November without the local streams freezing over, I never recall us getting far into December without all our water being locked up tight. There are no longer any migrating birds to watch. The deer have had to switch gears quickly from the intensity of the breeding season to the desperate need to feed. They attempt to enter the coming winter in the best possible condition. The breeding bucks have an especially urgent need, for they have spent themselves during last month's rut. The snowshoe hare and weasel have turned to their white winter color.

December is the month when my hunting winds down. I enjoy the winding down, which actually begins after the November deer season. I am not tired of hunting, but rather tired from hunting. In my house, I have a den. It is one room over which I have total control. From September through November, it is an unsightly and cluttered room. Every available counter space seems to be covered with the miscellaneous items the hunter depends on: ammunition, duck, goose and deer calls, flashlights, tree steps, and what have you. The deer antlers on the wall serve as hangers for tree-stand safety belts, socks, gloves, and a dozen other articles. During this winding down period, the den is put back together, organized and made to look like the quiet study of a sportsman as opposed to a supply dump. I enjoy getting the room organized again and evenings spent around the house. I can read a little and get ready for Christmas. I like to look at the photos and trophies in the room, and to remember. There may be a new, special photograph on the wall. If I am very lucky, there will also be a fresh set of antlers. In December, one can still hunt deer with archery tackle and the grouse and rabbit seasons are still open. For the most part, I take it easy, doing the occasional grouse or rabbit hunt. In 2001, however, I did little or none of those. For you see, I was still thinking about ducks.

Dolphins in the Decoys

Like so many other folks, I have made the Disney pilgrimage. In about 1987, my wife and I scrimped, saved and made the trip with the three kids. We flew to Orlando and purchased four-day passes to the legendary fantasy world. We also visited other family attractions. I rousted the family up each day to be at the chosen site as it opened. We usually stayed until it was ready to close. It was exhausting, but fun. It was as much fun for me as it was for the kids. I wanted to see it again, and my wife and I vowed we would return some day without the kids. We did this in 2000 to celebrate our twenty-fifth wedding anniversary. We had a great time, but the Magic Kingdom loses a little of its magic when there are no kids along to enjoy it. I realized I'd had enough of the Mouse to hold me for a long time.

Shortly after our return from this anniversary outing, a time-share outfit contacted us about coming down to stay at their facility. They would charge a ridiculously low price so they could have another chance at us with their skilled and persuasive sales folks. I was not too keen on this, but my better half thought it was a great idea. Our daughter and son-in-law also thought it would be fun and said they wanted to take a vacation with us. Always eager to keep the family in touch and having fun, I considered the idea. Then I remembered the stories I had read about duck hunting in Florida. I had read that the shooting around the space coast was terrific, and I knew a lot of ring necks and scaup wintered there. My son-in-law, Derek, has taken well to duck shooting since he began hanging around with my daughter and me, so I knew he would be up for it.

At first, the Alpha Female curled her lip at the thought of me going duck hunting during a family vacation trip. Then she realized it was probably the only way to get me enthusiastic about Orlando. Therefore, she thought it would be fine. I began searching for an outfitter. I had never paid someone to take me hunting before, but this time thought a guide was the only way to go. I would not be able to carry a duck hunting kit down there even if we drove. The gun, waders and blind bag each of us would need would be too much of a load when combined with the normal baggage one needs for a five-day trip across the country. I made contact with Captain Jeff Kraynik, who operates Florida Cracker Outdoor Adventures in Palm Bay, Florida, just a bit south of Cape Canaveral. We booked a morning duck hunt.

Always pinching pennies, we drove instead of flying. We left the day after Christmas. The plan was to push on straight to Florida, and with four drivers and only stopping when we or the car needed fuel, we made it to our destination in about thirty hours. I did manage to sneak in a brief tour of the Fred Bear Museum in Gainesville while the others snoozed in the car. I was a bit brain dead after the long hours in the car, but I just had to see this facility. When I was a boy, Fred Bear's hunts on The American Sportsman television series were something I marveled at. I had read his writings when I started bow hunting in the late 70s, and I knew of this museum. I had always hoped to be able to see it. See it I did, albeit through bloodshot and half-closed eyes.

We arrived on the 27th and I relaxed and did tourist stuff, waiting for our December 30 hunting date. When it finally arrived, we woke at 2:30 A.M. and drove east to meet Jeff. It was a ninety-minute drive, and we got to pass through some areas that were a bit quieter than most I had seen in Florida. We saw a few deer on the shoulders of the road.

We met Jeff at a convenience store and it was good to shake his hand and meet face to face after our many telephone conversations. Jeff is a full-time police officer in Palm Bay. His workweek is four ten-hour days, and he guides hunters, anglers, and nature lovers the other three days of the week. He has three other guides in his employ. He is a transplanted Ohioan who has been in Florida for about eighteen years. He is both personable and professional. He realized we were novices at diver shooting in general, and that we had never hunted the area. Our original plan had been to hunt puddle ducks on freshwater marshes near Cape Canaveral, but after the September 11 tragedy, much of that area was closed for security reasons. Instead, we hunted the Indian River Lagoon in Palm Bay. The water here is brackish but not subject to tidal changes. At the boat landing, we saw a sign cautioning boaters about manatees, so I asked Jeff what sea creatures we might see. He said the manatees were likely all out of the lagoon due to cooler weather. They like to move to power plant areas, where they find warm water discharges to bask in. However, dolphins are common and small sharks might be seen. He also instructed us on how to shuffle our feet along when wading so as not to step on stingrays. Evidently, if you bump them with your foot, they will swim off, but if you step on them, they are likely to throw up their tail and sting you. Then, Jeff said, he would have to remove the sting and piss on the wound. That would not add much fun to the hunt! I felt my toes curling in an effort to grip the ground beneath them.

We left the landing in the light of a full moon, occasionally shaded by thin and scattered clouds. The water of the lagoon was neither calm nor rough. The weather was warm by Minnesota standards, and it was not uncomfortable to motor along without hat or gloves. We traveled several miles and pulled up next to a mangrove island where we set out five dozen decoys. Most were on gang rigs of four to twelve decoys, and they were bluebill decoys. We also had some teal and black duck decoys rigged on individual weights. The nice-looking blocks were a brand I had never seen before, though just a little too heavy for my kind of canoe hunting where weight is a factor. Jeff did most of the work, with some assistance from Derek. We had a pleasant visit in the moonlight while the decoys were set up. When that chore was done, we pulled the boat up next to the island and covered up a bit.

We enjoyed that wonderful cup of coffee just before dawn, watching the distant lights along the shore and listening to the world wake up. We also talked to Jeff about what kind of birds we might see. He told us it would be mostly lesser scaup. The greater scaup was rare or non-existent here, at least during this time of year. I knew ringnecks wintered in Florida, but Jeff explained that these birds had certain areas with huge concentrations of "Ringers," but it was unlikely we would see any. Canvasbacks had recently migrated into the area, though, so there was a chance we would see those regal birds as well as widgeon, the two eastern species of teal, and the Florida Mallard. He said it was often an hour or more after sunrise when the birds began to fly.

We didn't have to wait that long to see birds. A few bills started to fly within minutes of legal shooting hours. None gave us a chance or even paid attention to our decoy spread. We did have three widgeon buzz us, coming from the rear, but they were out of range by the time we reacted. Then, a pair of Florida Mallards gave the decoys a look and passed by the outer edge of the spread. We all fired and I got feathers from the trailer but nothing came down. The shots were not as close as I like, but I have killed plenty of ducks at that range. There was no excuse for all three of us missing other than missing ducks is the easiest thing in the world to do.

With the bills paying no attention to our spread, Jeff decided to change locations. We waded out, picked up the blocks and moved a mile or so to a tiny island about six feet wide by twenty feet long. A single mangrove tree was growing at one end, and the boat fit nicely beneath it. We re-deployed the decoys and stood leaning against the boat, the tree providing good cover but still allowing shooting through openings between the limbs. It was a bit cloudy but warm, and the salty smell of the lagoon and mild breeze were pleasant. Dolphins played and hunted all around us. At times, they were within ten yards of the decoys. Jeff said the previous day a dolphin had tail-slapped one of the decoys and sent it flying thirty yards. His clients enjoyed that very much! One of those clients was a man on his first duck hunt, and while tracking an incoming bird, happened to pull the trigger just as the roboduck decoy came into the sight picture. He centered the decoy almost perfectly, and it was speckled with pellet holes. The decoy suffered some internal injuries as well. In spite of Jeff's best efforts to repair the wires, it would sporadically start and stop throughout our hunt. We finally concluded it was a union duck.

Our first opportunity to shoot from our new location came while Jeff was doing surgery on the roboduck. Derek, ever the mechanic, was watching and advising, when from my left, five bills buzzed right over the decoys. I got off a quick shot and missed, but the birds circled at Jeff's call and came back in. We folded one drake on their return. He was a beautifully colored lesser scaup. A few more small groups of birds checked out our decoy spread over the next hour, and we got a couple of more volleys in, getting three more drakes and one hen. All were with flocks of four to eight birds. The drakes were all in beautiful plumage.

We picked up at 10:30 and motored back to the landing. Jeff had some business to attend to, so Derek and I drove to a park in town to try to spot a manatee. We planned to meet Jeff for lunch and then head out for an afternoon dove shoot at his hunting club. We got a look at a manatee and could make out propeller scars on its flank.

We met Jeff for lunch at a local eatery and were joined by Jim, one of his guides. From there, we met two other clients from

Orlando and drove to the dove field, where perhaps a dozen other people showed up. We spread out to cover the field in hopes the birds would work to it in the evening. It was a gentlemen's hunt for sure, as we sat on stools in the warm afternoon sunshine and took a poke at the occasional dove that flew within range. I managed to kill one and there were about a dozen killed by the group that afternoon.

Thus ended our Florida hunt. The birds were not very plentiful, but the experience was well worth the time and money. It was another new experience and more new memories to add to the library. I got to smell the salt spray, which I had read about. Now, when I remember this hunt, or read about hunts on saltwater, this distinct smell will come back to me. Dolphins swimming around the decoys was something I had never imagined.

If I go to visit the Mouse again, I will reserve a day for another Florida duck hunt.

Truce

For several years in the late eighties and early nineties, we fed deer in our yard. Like most hunters, I persecute the game during the open season and try to insure its well-being for the rest of the year. A cyclic truce has been established. Feeding deer, according to the wildlife experts, is not feasible on a large scale as a measure to help them through the winter. We have known that for years. Today the experts caution us that feeding can concentrate the deer to an unhealthy level and actually hurt the herd by facilitating the spread of disease. Recently, there has been great concern about a disease called chronic wasting disease, and deer in neighboring Wisconsin have been infected. If I had been feeding deer this year that probably would have convinced me to stop. Our modest program years ago was done more for entertainment than anything else, though we hoped it might help the deer a bit too.

Beginning in October or early November, I would put occasional offerings of corn, horse feed, or actual deer feed, in the yard. After our firearm season closed, I began putting out small piles of feed each day when I arrived home from work. The deer in the neighborhood began to visit with increasing regularity. As they recovered from the pressure of the hunting season and grew accustomed to our yard, they became bolder. We moved the feed offerings closer and closer to the house or the powerful yard light I had mounted on the end of the garage. Usually, they began to move in at dusk and often each deer or group of deer would make several visits during the night. The horse feed had molasses in it and the deer definitely preferred this to the other two kinds. The deer feed was the least preferred. Most years they quit coming to feed in January. For whatever reason, the trip to the food pile was not worth the effort. We had no more dinner guests until spring when the snow was nearly gone. Then our visitors returned, usually bolder than ever. I have an aerial photo of the house and property taken during the spring of one of these deer-feeding years, when there was just a bit of snow on the ground. The deer trails can be seen reaching out from the yard, giving the appearance of a large open fan.

Our first year we had only three or four deer that would regularly come to feed. This number increased each year and peaked at about fifteen animals. During that year there were three bucks among the fifteen, including a beautiful nine-point. He was the first to arrive each night. When I arrived home from work, I would put out the deer food and go inside for supper. Before I was finished with my supper, the buck would have begun his. He generally came in once, fed, and was gone until the next evening. After he left, the procession would start. There were two spike bucks and the rest of the crew were does and fawns.

I never tired of watching these animals. After perhaps thirty evenings spent on deer stands through the bow and rifle season, much of that watching deer, I was still content to spend my non-hunting evenings watching deer. We turned the couch around (much to my wife's dismay) to face the picture window. That is where I sat after supper. My daughter shared my fascination and sat with me for hours, observing nature up close. She named each deer, the nine-point becoming known as Buster. It might surprise some people to learn that when one observes a group of deer over time, it becomes quite easy to recognize individuals. I think had any one of the fifteen regulars come in alone, Tara and I could have told you its name. With bucks, of course, each has distinctive antlers. The does and fawns have different body types and head shapes. Some of the fawns had noticeably thicker legs.

I enjoyed this deer watching immensely. I learned about deer society. Buster was, I think, the boss. However, he was usually there and gone before any of the others showed up. Buster and some of the others liked sunflower seeds. I watched him use his antlers to knock around a tube feeder, spilling seeds on the ground where he then gobbled them up. A huge doe, with a long body and long snout, was the next most dominant of our herd. When she and her twin fawns arrived all the others gave way. One of the spike bucks foolishly challenged her one evening. The big doe soundly thrashed him. As she reared up on her hind legs and kicked him furiously with her front hooves, chunks of his hair were sent flying through the air.

I set up the video camera on the tripod several times, using the timed exposure feature that took one second of video each minute. With the clock display on, I trained the camera on the lighted area where the feed was. I let the camera run overnight. Then I played back the tape and checked the times when the deer came and went. This is how I learned, without having to stay up all night, about their multiple nocturnal visits.

Over the holidays we generally have a lot of company. One year, while the feeding program was underway, we hosted a family Christmas party. Everyone got a treat seeing deer right in the yard, sometimes nibbling on corn placed on the porch steps. A few of the guests had little interest in the deer, but most would check regularly as to what was happening with the visitors in the yard. However, my brother-in-law, Bob, was awed.

Bob, at the time, was the owner of a successful business. He was a very busy man and lived in an urban area. I knew he liked nature. He was a fisherman, and he enjoyed watching a bird feeder set up outside his kitchen window. Our deer amazed him, and he joined us on that couch for a long time during our get together.

Years after our feeding program ended, each spring and fall, we would see groups of deer stop to look at the places where we had once placed food. These were usually does and fawns. I am sure the doe was an animal who had fed here years before, perhaps led there by her mother when she was less than a year old. One spring, some nieces and nephews were staying with us for a few days. They lived in a small town and seemed to enjoy getting a taste of country living. One evening, several deer walked into the yard well before sundown. The kids all jumped onto the couch and chattered with excitement. They were unaccustomed to having deer so close. I was in the kitchen, looking outside in the other direction. A great gray owl was perched on the electric pole in the yard. I called the kids over and showed them the owl. As we watched the huge bird, a skunk ambled down the driveway towards us. One of the girls looked up at me with wide eyes and asked,

"Uncle Dan, is it always like this here?"

I told her that a lot of the time it was. She thought I was very lucky.

She is right.

January

January in Northeast Minnesota can be brutal. While we never have the snowfall I was accustomed to in Upper Michigan, the temperatures can be terribly frigid. Nevertheless, after the holidays, which I spend hunting for food around the house, I am ready to get to the woods again. It is a time for watching the winter birds around the feeder. Each year we can count on certain kinds of birds to be there, and these common species seem to be around every day in about the same numbers from year to year. Other kinds may only appear one year in three. Still others may be rare one year and in great numbers the next. When I fed deer in the yard, they often abandoned my offerings in January and chose to stay in their winter hideaways out of the cold wind, rather than make a trip for some free corn. This month usually brings the bitterest cold of the year in one of the most bitterly cold parts of the country. It seems almost a miracle any wild thing can survive.

For many years, my January hunts were confined to rabbit hunting with my beagles. When I was really into hounding big time, every Saturday and Sunday, with few exceptions, were spent with the dogs in one of the countless swamps of Cedar Valley Township. One Saturday many years ago, I got up before daylight to hunt, and the temperature was thirty-eight degrees below zero. I sat in the kitchen drinking coffee until it warmed up to minus twenty. Then I went rabbit hunting. I was a diehard beagler, and often hosted small groups of friends and relatives to hunt over my pack, which had as many as five dogs. There were occasional years when the snow depth got to be too great for the dogs to work the rabbits very effectively. It was also difficult for the hunters to get around. Still, I found a way to get out for a few hunts each year. In recent years, I have fled the cold for a week to hunt ducks in the south.

The days begin to lengthen in late December, but I do not notice this until January. I have read about the "January thaw" that some areas enjoy now and again. I thought in my part of the world the January thaw came around just a little more often than Haley's Comet. However, the last several years we enjoyed some above-freezing temperatures during this month. I hope our average January weather does not return any time soon.

Release the Hounds

My two little hounds, Vinny and Annie had not been run in a while. This was Annie's first hunting season and she had been out of action for several weeks due to being in season and then with a badly cut foot. It was between five and ten degrees above zero, which is about as good as I can hope for in my neck of the woods at that time of year. So I got out my Ruger 10-22 and my hounds and walked out behind the house to do a little bunny hunting.

We began by working over some brush piles along side our main woods trail just a short distance from the house. Vinny pushed one out of one of the larger piles and I could have shot but let it go so the dogs could start a chase. This they did, but it only lasted about fifteen minutes before they lost the trail. I decided to head north, to my property line, and work the fence line around the west end of my land, bringing the dogs along and trying to put them into likely cover. With younger hounds, you often have to get involved in "striking game," which is simply jumping the rabbit out of its daytime bed.

We slowly worked around the property, to the field in the southwest corner of the place. We then skirted the edge of the field and headed along the edge of the cedar swamp that sits just north of this field. As we approached a pond I had excavated there, Vinny jumped a rabbit but even with the hot scent, he had trouble really opening on it. Annie joined him and did her best but the chase was slow and sporadic as they continually lost the trail. After ten or fifteen minutes of this, the dogs became separated, and then the Vin Man *opened up on hot scent for just a little bit, and then shut up again. Annie joined him and they picked up the scent, appeared to be a little confused at first, then opened beautifully together on the hot trail and began really moving that rabbit.*

Hunting over hounds is really a lot of fun. Their voices are sweet music to a lot of us and when you hear that baying swing around and come your way, your pulse quickens as you try to scan the brush for the approaching game. The rabbit usually gets by you without being seen, or if seen you often cannot get a shot. This is especially true when you hunt with a .22 instead of a shotgun. If you do get a shot, there is no guarantee you will hit the thing.

This particular rabbit got by me two or three times without being seen, passing close to me but in thick brush. Rabbits usually circle when being run by hounds, so your strategy is to get close to a place where the rabbit has already run and where you have decent visibility. Then you hope the hounds can stay with it long enough to bring it by that spot again. You must be careful when you move around, because the rabbit can be several minutes ahead of the hounds and if he sees or hears you, he may start running a different route. What you do is wait until the dogs are at the far side of the circle from you and then make your move. That is exactly what I did now, moving into the thick swamp and taking up a position standing on the upturned roots of a wind-thrown cedar. I could see a couple of different places where the dogs and rabbit had come through on the previous circles, deep troughs cut through the foot deep snow by the hard-working beagles. I heard the dogs begin to come my way.

It took just a few minutes. I saw the rabbit bouncing along, quartering towards me. The brush and deep snow saw to it that I didn't get much of a look, just glimpses of him zipping along. The .22 is scope sighted which complicates this type of situation even more, but it is darn good practice for picking up a moving target in the scope. Finally, I had a longer look and shot but I knew my swing had not caught up to the bunny and I shot behind him. I followed him in the scope as best I could and got a second shot that was good in the horizontal, but went over or under him. The third shot felt right. If you have done this, you know what I mean. I don't know if you see the hit or maybe just get a good look at the sight picture at the instant of the shot and can't register it the normal way or what. Maybe that adrenaline-

rich condition wipes out your conscious memory of what you saw, but the feeling of success stays. I don't know the scientific explanation but sometimes, you just feel like you have done it right.

I brought the gun down and looked for movement but saw none. I hopped down off my lookout and walked over to where the bunny had last been seen. There he was, giving his last kicks, shot through the eye. The dogs arrived about then, and we celebrated a bit for the good efforts we had all made. We then moved on to check some more brush piles.

Soon Vinny started a rabbit from under a blow-down and Annie joined him on the trail. This was a tough trail and they were quiet as much as they were giving voice. I climbed up on another blowdown where I could see well and waited a long time for the dogs to make a circle, due to the problems they were having with this trail. Finally, though, I saw the rabbit hopping along and stopping every few feet. At about thirty-five yards I shot—offhand and standing on a narrow log. The rabbit flopped over and when I picked him up, he was within six feet of the bed where Vinny had jumped him. With two rabbits in hand, I had now equaled the best day ever with these two new hounds. I was proud of the work they did on this last trail, sticking with the tough scent trail until the rabbit came around to me.

We moved back to the area where we had originally started this hunt and the dogs jumped one quickly. This rabbit took a straight line for a couple of hundred yards before he started to circle. I held my position for a while thinking he would come back. When that didn't happen, I moved towards the chase. The rabbit crossed into the neighbor's land, back to mine, and led the dogs on this circle a couple of times. Annie saved the day twice by picking up tough checks. (A check occurs when the dog loses the scent) I was standing on the south side of the largest of the four ponds in our woods, when the dogs passed to the east of me, heading north. They then turned west and as they passed straight north of me, a rabbit popped up over the berm on the far side of the pond. He was headed towards me and I shot twice, turning the rabbit back the way he had come. It disappeared over the berm, then suddenly popped up fifteen feet to the right, and again headed towards me. I started shooting, the little .22 auto giving its little "peck, peck, peck," but having no effect on the rabbit. He ducked into thick brush fifteen yards from me, then emerged twenty yards away, now headed east and straightaway from me. I

was down to the last round in the ten shot clip and it rolled him. When I followed the back trail, I found my first or second shot had hit him and at least one other. This rabbit turned out to be a stray, that is, not the rabbit the dogs were trailing but one that was moved by the nearby chase. The dogs were still on that original rabbit and I now moved to a six or seven-year-old aspen cutting, right in the center of the property.

The dogs moved the rabbit in and around the two-acre cutting that was now thick with ten to fifteen foot tall aspen. The dogs lost the trail for several minutes, and this happened once or twice before I glimpsed the quarry a couple of times with no luck getting a shot. Then another stray showed up, hopping quickly into the cuttings from neighboring balsams. My first shot missed, but he stopped at the shot. I had to lean around some intervening brush to take the second shot and it appeared I had missed. As I squeezed off the third shot though, I noticed him already starting to sink down. The last two shots hit the neck area and rabbit number four for the day was in hand.

I gathered up my two young partners and headed home. I was extremely pleased with the two young hounds for the way they stuck with their trailing in spite of very difficult conditions. Most of the chases that day had been very difficult, but they just worked and worked until the rabbit came around and, thankfully, I was able to make the shots.

Four snowshoe hare are not exactly like a grand slam on mountain sheep, I will admit, but the hunt just described was extremely satisfying for me. The two young dogs I had trained myself had, with my help, done the hard work to move four bunnies to the gun. Considering their age and the conditions, it was a very good showing. This was a hunt to remember—not for the game taken, but for the effort involved in taking that game.

The Grand Prairie

Today I am not the die-hard beagler I was years ago. I still have one of the little hounds, but she is more of an ornament than a hunting companion. While I still pursue the big northern hares on occasion, beginning in 1997, my January hunting efforts turned to duck hunting in the great state of Arkansas.

If you follow duck hunting in America, you know about Arkansas. Stuttgart, in the east central part of the state, is near where the Mississippi, White and Arkansas rivers converge. In this same area, there are numerous bayous and tributaries to each of these major rivers. It is a natural funnel to migrating waterfowl and the ancestral wintering grounds for many of these birds, particularly mallards. The timbered river bottoms flood here at this time of year, naturally or with the help of man, and the agricultural land is mostly used to farm rice, beans or winter wheat. Waterfowl have adapted well to using these fields for feeding and loafing, so the landscape brings in the ducks, and the ducks bring in the duck hunters. Stuttgart is the epicenter. It is the home of the World Duck Calling Championship and of Mack's Prairie Wings, which is the largest waterfowling store I have ever seen. Each November, Stuttgart holds their Wings over the Prairie festival, which is a celebration of duck hunting.

The Stuttgart area lies in what is called the Grand Prairie, an area of prairie that occurs naturally in the midst of the forested lands that once covered most of the state. The Grand Prairie encompasses an area twenty miles wide by a hundred miles long. It had once teemed with game including clouds of prairie grouse. This area lent itself well to crop farming, and in particular, rice farming, which began around the turn of the century. The virgin soil was tilled, and today there is less than 100 acres left of that natural prairie. Also gone are the grouse and other grassland species that thrived here, but replacing them are ducks and geese in untold thousands.

In January 1997, I got the idea of taking a trip there to check what all the duck hunting fuss was about. The Alpha Female, the dog and I, took a trip down. Some folks we knew from our hometown of Floodwood had moved to Hazen, Arkansas (twenty miles from Stuttgart) several years before. We stopped to see them and they would not let us leave! Thus started one of the most special friendships my wife and I have—with Bob and Judy Juola. Judy has family from that area and introduced me to her cousin, Phillip Boothe, who is (as Judy put it) exactly like me in his love of hunting and the outdoors. Thus began another friendship that endures to this day. I have many fine companions who I share hunts with, and none finer than Mr. Phillip Boothe. He is a friend and kindred spirit.

My annual trip to Arkansas is special for many reasons. I doubt there is anywhere in America with better duck shooting. Still, there are many places a man can go to get good shooting. For me, Arkansas has a lot more to offer. I can escape the Minnesota winter for a bit during its toughest month and spend time with my Arkansan friends. I also enjoy the friendly hospitality of the rural south and the general good nature of its people. There is plenty of public hunting land, and my contacts there have gotten me access to some great private land hunts as well. In addition, there is Carol's Kitchen.

Carol's Kitchen is a small Mom-and-Pop type restaurant on the east end of Hazen's main street. It was where I started my first Arkansas duck hunt and it was my last stop in Hazen this past January. It is nicely decorated with many flavors of décor, including mounted ducks and wildlife art. Its busiest time (as far as I have seen) is between five and seven in the morning. That is when farmers, cops, game wardens and duck hunters pile in to have breakfast, socialize and conduct intelligence gathering. In the case of the hunters, it is also a place to rendezvous with other members of their party for the day. The dominant topic of conversation is duck hunting, and camouflage clothes outnumber all other types about ten to one. It is a very congenial atmosphere. If you need to refill your coffee cup, you get up and do it yourself, and then you walk around with the pot to see if anyone else needs a refill. When I get to Carol's each morning, it feels almost like home.

I arrived in Hazen on January 14 this past year, about two in the afternoon. I popped in to visit with Judy for a bit and then went to their shop to say hello to Bob and his brother Tim. I drove down to Stuttgart to check out Mack's Prairie Wings and picked up a case of shotgun shells for myself, and one for Phillip. I had supper at Carol's, then it was back to Bob and Judy's to wait for Phillip. When he arrived about six, we headed to his place, where he had his rather spacious travel trailer set up in the yard for me to stay in.

The hunting had been very slow for almost the entire season. Mild weather to the north allowed the ducks to linger in those areas, and the normal influx of northern birds was greatly reduced. There had also been a lot of water that winter, which allowed the birds that were there to spread out. There were many rather glum duck hunters; in particular, the guides, who need their clientele to have good shooting. As for me, I was just happy to be somewhere with an open season. I didn't need many birds to make me happy, and I was sure I would have hunting as good, or better, than what I was used to in Cedar Valley.

Most of the local hunters list flooded timber hunting as their favorite type of duck shooting. We tried that our first couple of days and it was pretty slow. Rice field hunting is the next most popular, but the fields we had access to were not holding many ducks. However, Phillip and I were keen to hunt, and we were both willing to work at it. Phillip knew the country well, and we soon began to scout the countryside to find huntable numbers of birds. It did not take us long to find some, either. Phillip and his friends lease approximately 1500 acres for deer hunting. The lease includes a rice field and a beaver slough, formed by a series of dams. In one spot there is a huge beaver flooding. It was in this slough and the beaver pond that we started finding many ducks. Perhaps it wasn't a lot by Arkansas standards, but it was enough to keep us interested. Then, by mid-week, the ducks and geese began using the rice field. We spent most of the last four days of my hunt on the deer lease, hunting all three of the areas mentioned. Our morning visits to Carol's revealed we were killing as many or more ducks than anyone, so we couldn't ask for more than that.

I could tell about the entire week, but I won't. What I will do is tell about the most unforgettable day of that week, because it ranks as one of my most unforgettable hunting days ever. A day we began in the big beaver flooding.

We drove in the predawn darkness to the deer lease and parked our trucks in the camp yard. There we loaded our decoys and gear onto Phillip's three-wheeled ATV and drove to the beaver flooding a mile away. We had to wade a couple of hundred yards through shallow water to the opening in the flooded grass where we planned to set up. The previous afternoon we had found some birds here and managed to shoot a few. It took us longer than anticipated to set up, and by the time we were ready to hunt, several minutes of legal shooting time had passed. All the while we were preparing, we had birds overhead. It did not take long for our first customer to arrive, a lone greenhead that decoyed beautifully and tumbled into the spread at my shot. A second suffered the same fate a few minutes later, and then a trio came to look us over. Phillip and I both shot at the lead green-head, taking him down, and each crediting the other with the kill. After that, it got slow. There were plenty of birds but they would not work to us. Phillip was ready to call it quits on the morning hunt but I stayed. He planned to come back for me about eleven with some food. We would have lunch at the deer camp and rest for a bit. When it was time to start the evening hunt, we would move to the rice field.

It was a sunny and pleasant day. I enjoyed the quiet wait on the slough but killed no other birds, missing a couple of longer shots. When I picked up the decoys and hauled them out, Phillip was waiting for me.

We adjourned to the camp and had some lunch. Phillip then napped in one of the buildings while I took my rest in a sunny spot in the yard. Sleep would not come. I walked to the slough, a hundred yards down the hill from camp, with Jill and my shotgun. We had been jumping some birds here earlier and in fact, had walked down when we first got to camp that afternoon to listen for ducks. We had heard none then, but now I heard mallards on the water. I listened for a long time, trying without success to locate them. I began to move along the edge of the slough and across the beaver dam. Part way across, I heard the feeding calls. Now I had them located. They were in some buck brush, but I could not see them and there was no reason for them to come out in the open. I decided to try to give them a reason and sent Jill in swimming after them with a "Hunt 'em up!" command.

Watching a good dog work is one of the greatest joys in the joyful pastime of hunting. Jill is a pretty good dog. She has some faults, but I blame my lack of experience as a trainer for these. She is intelligent, has an exceptional nose and is persistent. I can't count the times she has done amazing things for me in the field. At my command, she followed the hand signal, and soon I could see she had scent. It was obviously quite a puzzle for her as she swam back and forth, a bit confused by the scent. The ducks had been in this slough for hours, and the dog would have to unravel their meandering, in that almost supernatural way they seem to do. Finally, she swam off on a straight-line course, locked on to hot scent. Moments later, I heard the sound of ducks jumping. There were a half-dozen of them, and as soon as I saw them above the buck brush, it was obvious they were not going far. They were out of range, so I did not shoot. They circled away from me and immediately landed again. I could hear them chuckling and fretting over the disturbance and could hear Jill moving around in the water where they had jumped. Then, the golden head of my favorite hunting partner and foot-warmer

came out of the buck brush, swimming for all she was worth in pursuit of the flock. There was a bend in that area of open water, and the ducks had landed just around this bend. The dog followed and soon there was the sound of a single bird getting up. It was a greenhead and it came round the bend right for me. There was a large "limby" tree right in front of me. As the duck bore down on me, I raised the gun and swung onto the target. He was very close and now a maze of limbs was in my sight picture. I touched off a shot and could see that at least part of the pattern barked one of the limbs, but the duck splashed down dead, less than ten yards from me. The rest of the flock flushed and went out the other end of the slough. I called Jill over to retrieve the bird, for which she truly deserved full credit.

I returned to the camp yard and got some photos of the four greenheads we had. Phillip slept through my hunt but was up shortly afterwards. About 2:00 P.M., his friend, Rusty Rogers, who I had met and heard a lot about but had never hunted with, joined us. We set out for the rice field and our evening hunt.

We set up decoys in one corner of the rice field. Phillip left Rusty and I there and headed out on his ATV for the slough, intending to jump shoot there and move birds out, that hopefully, would see our decoys and find some interest in them.

As soon as Phillip got into the slough, birds began to leave, and many came towards us. A Suzy worked the decoys and I got her with my second shot. Birds were all over the skies and we lay on the levee keeping our faces down, hoping they would work to our calling and decoys. Rusty was doing the calling and we had birds above us when I heard the distinctive peep of a pintail drake. I have hoped for a pintail (sprig) or canvasback ever since I began traveling to Arkansas. The birds are in much better plumage in January than they are during the Minnesota season. I wanted a "mounter." Now, I had a pintail overhead. Rusty worked the mallard call and I whistled back at the pintail. Shortly, two birds came in from downwind. It was a pintail pair. The pintail drake is the most graceful bird on the wing that you will ever see. Their wings were locked and feet down. The spiked tail was obvious and the sun lit up his beautiful colors. It was a "gimme" shot, the sort of decoy-shot you see in the videos and paintings and that you pray for. I got up and got the gun on him. I pulled the trigger and got a click. I had fired on an empty chamber.

I had other shells in the gun and had I just pumped the action quickly, I would have had an easy shot. But the surprise of the situation froze me for a split second, and rattled the heck out of me. I am sure it was only a second or two, but when I pumped in a shell and finally took the shot, I missed. It was my first ever chance at a pintail and I had blown it. Rusty got to see my true personality then, as I set to wailing and gnashing my teeth. Of course, he didn't know of my desire for a bull sprig, but I soon explained the situation. He chuckled. Such is hunting.

We resumed our positions and only a few minutes later, as I looked to the right, I heard the whistle of wings over the decoys. I turned, just as another beautiful pintail was leaving range after giving the decoys a look. Had I been alert, it would have been a reasonably good shot. I wailed some more and Rusty chuckled some more.

It was only a few minutes later when more birds were circling overhead. There were singles and doubles and small bunches, including a group of about a dozen that contained both sprig and mallards. There were at least two pintail drakes in the group. They peeped at the decoys, and I peeped back. We had to keep our faces down and look out the corner of our eyes, under the bills of our caps, to watch as the birds circled right over us. I knew if a mallard gave us a chance first, Rusty would take it. I hoped the first thing in would be a pintail drake.

As I peered out over the decoys, a pair of mallards came into view, locked up and coming to the spread. I didn't even have time to cuss my luck as just to one side (more near me) and a bit higher, a pintail pair appeared. They too were locked, and coming in.

It is customary and proper etiquette, when a flock is coming in, to wait until there are birds for your partner to shoot at before you, yourself, pull up to shoot. That way both hunters have a chance. I did not consider the etiquette question. When that buck pintail was where I thought I could get him, I came up shooting. He folded with my first shot. It was great! Rusty didn't get a shot but he got a comedy show, because when my bird hit the shallow water of the rice field, I was up and running to him. I told Jill to sit and stay, which she usually does without question or fault. However, she had never seen this exact scenario before. With a duck down and her master sprinting out to retrieve, she broke and ran out with me. I shouted orders for her to sit. She would pause, break, and I would shout again. Then the whole routine would repeat. She is not a hard-mouthed dog, but I wanted to pick this bird up gently, and personally. I was so charged up that I am sure I looked even more ridiculous than I usually do.

The bird had its head up and when I got close, he began to flutter away. Now I gave Jill the fetch command and followed at a run. The poor dog was now really confused, but when in doubt, she fetches. She chased down the bird and she pinned it. I immediately grabbed my pintail.

I apologized to Rusty for jumping on the shot, but he just laughed. I guess the comedy show was better than getting a duck. He asked if I was ever gonna come back, now that I had my pintail. I joked that when Phillip returned, I would tell him I had my pintail and I was heading home in the morning, never to return.

When you have success in hunting that was long sought and fairly won, it is a feeling that cannot be described. I lay there on that levee in the rice stubble, my trophy at my side, the sun shining on him and showing his beautiful plumage. It was cool, breezy and bright, and my spirits were high. It was all I could have asked for. However, much to my delight, there was more to come.

We knew this rice field had only recently started pulling in some ducks and geese. The geese were mostly snows, but also large numbers of specklebellies were in the area as well as Canada geese. After shooting the pintail, I can't even remember if we shot at any more ducks, though I know we did not kill anymore. An hour or so before dark, we saw and heard a large flock of snow geese approaching. They came from our right, out of the north. We did not get too excited as huge flocks of snows are common here at this time of year, even though this trip I had seen fewer than usual. We watched as the flock approached, and as the leaders grew closer and closer, the far end of the flock was still somewhere out of sight beyond the horizon. I glanced at Rusty and he grinned, shook his head and declared that this might get interesting. On they came. As they approached our decoy spread, they turned to avoid us. I don't know if they did not like the decoys or could see the dog or us, but they definitely avoided our location. They began to circle and land in the far end of the field, a quarter-mile away. The noise was incredible as the evening sky was filled with their calls, and still the end of the flock was not in sight. They began to land.

Rusty and I grinned at each other and whispered back and forth. I wanted my camera but it was in a pocket covered by my waders. We lay still and peeked out from under our caps at the vortex of white and gray. It was stunning. They were landing and filling the field beginning at the far end. As more and more birds touched down, we could hear a sound like that of a rapids or waterfall. I can only guess that this was the sound of them beginning to feed in the shallow water. I estimate at least 200 birds per minute were landing and the vortex above the field was not changing in size. The flock still stretched back out of site over the horizon. Five minutes went by and still they came. Ten minutes. Fifteen minutes and the only change was the numbers of geese on the ground. The river of geese in the sky still reached beyond the horizon.

"Be ready when Phillip comes back on that three wheeler," said Rusty with a wide grin. I have seen many incredible sights in the outdoors and this was as awe inspiring as any of them. The noise was unbelievable. It seemed as though even the dog was awed, as she did not whine or fidget. Like Rusty and me, she just watched.

Then, for a second, we heard the ATV. Only for a second. Phillip came out of the trail and drove towards us. The flock was between him and us. When the birds saw the ATV, they started to get up. They gave their alarm calls, and it was deafening. I wish I could estimate how many birds there were. Five thousand? Ten thousand? I can't say. However, those that had been on the ground were up and moving towards us. Just as they did when they arrived, they began to swing wide of us. The closest were still in extreme range and we came up shooting. We emptied our guns and only one bird fell, but Jill got her first taste of snow goose as Phillip drove up laughing.

We laughed and talked about the geese for a long time and I showed Phillip my trophy pintail. He was properly impressed and congratulated me. He hid the wheeler, and we sat until dusk. We killed nothing, and I can't even remember if we shot. This day had been full of good things, especially the evening. I will never forget it. In fact, that evening in the trailer I started to record the day's events in my journal. I was bone tired but smiling. This is a common feeling for me after a day in the field. I wrote in detail about the day, but only got as far as the midday events around the camp. Then, I just penned in that in the evening, we hunted the rice field. I jotted down the number and kind of birds we had killed. I then hit the sack. I knew I could write down the events of the evening hunt much later, for they were too indelibly etched in my mind to forget.

I hunted seven days during this trip. Many of them were very full days with morning and evening hunts, as well as some mid-day hunts. We did well. I took twenty ducks and two geese, which included my fist-ever speckle belly goose and first snow goose. I killed an even better pintail a day or two after that first one, and that day we had pintails all over us. You can only take one per day. I was happy with the two lovely drakes. The pintails were the high point of the trip. Maybe that flock of geese was the high point. Maybe it was the time spent with Phillip and his family. Nice to be unsure about what part was the best.

Before I left Hazen, I stopped at Carol's Kitchen and took a photograph of a pair of mounted pintails that grace the wall there. I had admired this mount for years. I had two frozen pintail drakes in the truck. They would be delivered to a Minnesota taxidermist as soon as I got back home. I would also give him a copy of the photo as a guide to how I wanted my trophies mounted. When finished, they will have a place of distinction on the wall of our family room. Each time I stop to look at them, I will remember a breezy evening on an Arkansas rice levee. I will remember how the pintail drakes dropped into the decoys on cupped wings. And that living river of geese in the sky.

February

In February, we folk from northern Minnesota start to breathe easier, for February is the month when we usually begin to believe that winter really does end. Though it is not at all unusual to see the very bitter cold and snow of winter during the month, we can almost always count on the temperatures moderating by month's end. We normally get our January thaw in February. The days are now longer and there is time to do things after work in the daylight. You can almost count on regularly seeing some daytime high temperatures in the high teens and twenties. In February of 2002, we had the unusual treat of temperatures well above freezing, more days than not, during the month. One day in mid-month we hit fifty degrees. Another day it was raining at five o'clock in the afternoon. The snow depth in our woods was only about six inches and the winter was tame indeed. Little did we know we were being set up, for March was an entirely different story. However, in February, it hardly seemed like winter.

Except for the keenest of observers, there is little noticeable change in the behavior of the wildlife from that which we see in the earlier winter months. Real students of nature know that this month, the first stirrings of the mating season occur in some of our resident critters. Now is the time when coyotes breed. The snowshoe hare seem to be on the move now, perhaps getting to know potential mates. If your dog begins to chase one of these roaming rabbits, he may soon be out of hearing.

For most hunters here in Minnesota, the guns have been in storage since the end of the rifle deer season in November. Dedicated small game hunters will pursue the rabbits beyond that date, but as February ends, so does the rabbit season. Only a few dedicated varmint hunters will take to the Minnesota woods after February. There are the "non-consumptive" types, the skier and the snowmobile enthusiast, who will also be out. Then there is the rarest of all—those who hunt for knowledge, beauty, and a breath of fresh air.

Release the Hounds II

When I was doing a lot of rabbit hunting, it was during February that a subtle sign of the impending spring would show itself. The dogs would often take a rabbit's trail and the bunny would head out cross-country instead of circling as they normally would. Sometimes the trail ran for a mile or more that way before the rabbit settled down into the normal circular route. Other hound men I know have noticed the same thing and come to the same conclusion. We think the rabbits begin to roam outside their normal home range as they feel the first stirrings of the mating urge. I don't know much about rabbit biology, but in many ways, their behavior is much like whitetail deer. My thought is that the male rabbits begin to roam in search of females. If not to mate at this time, it is to learn their locations for future mating. This is what a whitetail buck will do during the pre-rut time when the does are not ready to breed. Those long-distance runners that lead the dogs a long way cross-country are (in my opinion) these male rabbits that have been caught outside their home area. When pushed by the dogs they make a beeline for familiar territory. This would explain the long sprint followed by the circling that I think begins when the rabbit has made it back to his home turf. I could be all wet, so if you have another explanation, I would love to hear it.

Each February, I try to work in one last rabbit hunt. The season closes on the last day of the month, which is sort of a birthday

gift to my wife who was born on March 1. This hunt is what I consider the last hunt of the year. I will hunt crows a couple of times when that season begins and perhaps try to bag a fox or coyote with my new electronic call. I have made one spring hunting trip for snow geese and several trips for turkey. Still, on the last day of February, I consider the hunting year to end. The guns and gear are stowed away. The den is in good order. I read, write and remember the season just passed. But getting back to that last rabbit hunt, this year's was a total fizzle. Toby, the better hunter of my two hounds, had moved to my daughter's home. Starr, our "ornamental" beagle, was all the canine help I could muster. I tried it, for old time sake, but she mostly snuffled along within thirty yards of me and never started a rabbit. For the story of a real season finale, I need to go back to February of 2001 and the journal entry I recorded describing that year's final outing.

February 24, 2001

My two beagles are not the best hounds I have ever owned, but I really don't know how good or how bad they are because I have hunted over them so little. Toby is nine and he was coming into his own as a hunter about the time I got away from obsessive rabbit hunting. His second and third seasons were years of very heavy snowfall and I just never got out with him. He is a tough little buggar, having survived a number of near death experiences, including a coyote snare and a car. He has a lot of scars and many aches and pains, but sometimes on a good day when the scent is holding, he runs like a puppy. It just takes him a while to recover afterwards. Starr was my daughter's pet and I never worked with this dog at all on hunting. She just picked up trailing rabbits on her own like many beagles do. She is overweight and her real specialty is getting into garbage, either in the garage or in the cupboard under the sink.

Both dogs live in the house. Starr always has and Toby got to move in when he was about three. Both of them have the world by the tail and hounding rabbits for their master is not one of their high priorities. When they feel like hunting, they hunt, and on occasion, they will pound the rabbits for eight, ten or twelve hours without interruption. When I take them out to hunt with me, it seems to confuse them a little. It is as if they think I am taking them for a walk, and they do not seem interested in hunting. This is my own fault because I have not shown them how much fun it is for us to hunt TOGETHER. Consequently, I have shot only the occasional rabbit in front of these two.

The snow this year is much deeper than it has been since 1997; deep enough that the dogs and I would all have some trouble getting around. Directly behind the house, however, the dogs had already been on a couple of their hunting expeditions. They had run the rabbits enough to have quite a network of trails packed down to the point that they would be able to get around okay. As for myself, I strapped on the snowshoes and began hoofing it around. I walked my own trail network and elsewhere, just to have a trail broken. When I hunted, it would be on snowshoes and I would be able to get around about anywhere with some effort, but with the network of broken trails, I could move along with much less effort. I decided I would hunt with my dad's old Winchester pump .22, the one I had learned to shoot with. Dad has been gone for a lot of years, but carrying that old gun and using the snowshoes that were also his would be as close as I could get to having him along. The *gun and the snowshoes were pieces of equipment that have been around longer than I have. It is always somewhat nice, for me at least, to have and use things that have just "always been there."*

The week dragged slowly at the office. We were working ten-hour days and I had scheduled work for Saturday as well, but I could put my time in on the weekend whenever it was convenient. I watched the weather reports closely. It was the final weekend of the season and I did not want the weatherman to ruin it for me. On Thursday the forecast was for temperatures in the high twenties on Saturday and snow starting in the morning and getting heavier by nightfall. These were auspicious signs. Before a heavy snow, the game might move more than usual. Temperatures above twenty usually meant better scenting conditions for the dogs, and the absolute best trailing I had ever seen my dogs do was when there were fluffy snowflakes coming down and no wind. Would I be lucky enough to see that set of conditions?

As I waited for Saturday, I reminisced about past hunts. Back in the sixties when I was in high school, I hunted with my pal Gary, his dad and their dog Sam. I still remember the Pike Lake hunt. It was the first time in my young hunting career that I was actually in on a major hunting success. We killed ten rabbits and I believe I got three of them. At that stage of my life, just coming home with something was a big success and coming home with more than one game bird or animal had happened only a couple of times. Here I was with three rabbits and my partners had done as well or better. It was heady stuff.

Then there were the big hunts in the late 1970s with my pack of five and all my brothers-in-law at "slaughterhouse." This was a narrow strip of swampy woods between a county road and a power-line. It was about a hundred yards wide and a mile and a quarter long. We would start at one end—walking abreast—and turn the dogs loose. As we worked our way along we would kick up a rabbit or two and get shots, or sometimes the dogs would run one back to us, but the bulk of the shooting took place near the far end. The rabbits naturally moved ahead of us and the dogs followed. Finally, as we moved down near the end of the alley, the rabbits were pinned in a smaller area. They began to trickle back through our skirmish line. That's when the shooting got intense. I remember getting twenty-seven and twenty-eight rabbits with the group on consecutive weekends.

There were other memorable hunts with a lot fewer rabbits killed. A late season hunt with my brother-in-law, Roger, in deep snow and tough conditions, where the dogs worked well and we worked our butts off in the deep snow to come home with five. There was another late season hunt, when it was just two young dogs and I. The trailing conditions were very poor. Instead of the constant baying of the dogs as they pushed the rabbit hard, it was one of those days where they would lose the trail often and for a long time. Nevertheless, they stuck with it and occasionally were howling on the trail for ten or fifteen minutes without interruption. I shot well with the .22, getting a couple as they came by on a dead run and another that was stationary but a long way off. We came home with four in four hours. That was one of those days where man and dog had to work hard and be at their best if any were to succeed, and darned if we didn't all come through for each other.

Any hunter lucky enough to have spent time hunting with dogs will remember them. At least he will remember the best ones, the worst ones, and the unique ones. As a kid, my first hunts were with two mongrels, my Tramp and my cousin's Smokey. Then there was Gary's Sam, of course. My Homer was the first dog I owned in Minnesota. I worked hard with him and he was a good one. Homer was named for a hound I had read about in Erwin Bauer's *Outdoor Life* writings. I also had a Sam, named after Gary's dog. My Sam was an incredible trailer on bare ground but could not handle snowy conditions. Suzy, who gave us several litters of pups, Fritz, who was the best of them and Vinny, who would have been, if he had lived long enough. He disappeared in the big Halloween blizzard in the early 1990s. I remember going to comfort my daughter when she went to bed. The blizzard was howling and Vinny was missing. I saw Tara's worried look—she was twirling her hair with her finger. I went in, sat on her bed and gave her a hug. She looked at me and said, "I don't want him to be gone, Dad." I hugged her, and though I did not say it, I didn't want him to be gone either.

There was Buster, who started out like a prodigy but then got to where he would back-trail them, heading the wrong way down the tracks. He could entertain himself for a long time on a hundred feet of scent because he would just keep running it back and forth. Blizzard was knock-kneed but he would run rabbits so long and so hard and with such enthusiasm, he whipped the end of his tail into a bare and bloody stump. His feet would also bleed.

It is obvious I get a lot of mileage out of one rabbit hunt each winter. Just getting ready for it has me reliving forty years of rabbit hunts. That is one of the obvious signs of advancing age. We don't get out and actually do much, but we will reminisce the heck out of things.

Thursday afternoon, we got those big fluffy snowflakes that make me want to get out behind the beagles. The TV weather people could not decide when our snowstorm would arrive. I hoped their original estimated time of arrival, Saturday afternoon, would prove correct so I could get my hunt in on that morning.

Friday dawned cold and mostly clear with no snow in the air. The weather folks were still noncommittal on the exact time the snow would arrive. At four in the afternoon the sun was still shining, but clouds and gray skies were starting to move in. Being a 21st century rabbit hunter, I logged onto my computer and connected to the Internet and then on to a local weather page. Here I found a forecast detailing conditions by the hour for the upcoming eight hours. It told me the clouds would keep moving in, but there was no snow mentioned in the outlook between four and eleven o'clock. The animated maps looked less encouraging though, with the clouds and precipitation shown moving from the central plains north, east, and already tickling the southwest corner of Minnesota. It looked certain I would be hunting in falling snow in the morning. Whether it would be the big, fluffy flakes floating straight down that seemed to make for good rabbit hunting, or horizontal sleet that made for poor hunting, was yet to be seen. I would hunt in either case, but for how long and with how much success would be determined in large part by the timing of the storm's arrival.

The beeping of the alarm clock gave me a start at six. Half asleep still, I tried to figure out what day it was. When I realized it was Saturday, I felt that little surge of excitement that comes when you realize you are going hunting instead of to work. Funny how much easier it was for me to get out of bed. My canine hunting partners were stretched out in the same bed I was—pampered little beasts compared to the dogs I had years before. Sleepily I made my way down the hall and to the back door, where I flipped on the porch light and anxiously checked the weather. There was about three or four inches of fresh snow and a few flakes coming down. Light winds from the southeast. It would do.

There was plenty of time. Shooting light was still nearly an hour away. While it's not really too important to get out early when hunting snowshoe hare, I wanted that slight advantage of getting out at first light when the nocturnal wanderings of my prey had just ended. This might let us stumble on fresh scent right away and get the dogs going. I did not want them to get caught up in just going for a walk with me; I wanted them to hunt. In my vision of the perfect hunt, they would find scent quickly and have a good chase for five or ten minutes and then I would kill the rabbit in front of them and let them worry it a bit. This would fill them with blood lust and set the tone for a wonderful day of dog work and a test of my marksmanship. A fella can dream, right?

The coffee cooked as I made some toast and ate it with a glass of milk. The dogs came out to see what I was doing but were pretty clueless. Not like my retriever or my beagles of old, who sensed an upcoming hunt and paced nervously as they watched me get ready.

"Well, I can't blame you that you're both spoiled house pets," I said aloud. They had the blood in them to be hunters and it was my lack of interest that had turned them into pets first and hunters second.

The second cup of coffee was almost as good as the first and I gathered my gear. I had closed the bedroom door and now the beagles sat by it looking forlornly at me as if begging to be let back in bed. I laughed. The toast and coffee were settled nicely when I stepped out and strapped on the antique snowshoes and headed west out of the yard along my nicely packed snowshoe trail. Starr was on a long leash. This was to make sure she would at least start looking for rabbits in a place of my choosing, instead of her own. Toby was not leashed, as I was quite sure he would follow along. Jill, the retriever, yipped at us in protest at being left behind.

We crossed the field and entered the woods, following the winding logging road that—in winter—was our ski trail. I unleashed Starr and turned off the main trail and on to one of my secondary trails that was just wide enough to walk through comfortably. I had snow-shoed here, so the going was easy. I stopped and loaded the ancient .22. It has a tube magazine and I filled it, hearing the familiar staccato clicking as the spring-loaded magazine tube was pushed back in and seated. I worked the slide and marveled again at how tight and solid the action was after sixty years or so of hard use. The heavy sounding "Kla-click" as the breechblock closed. This gun was built right, and it was like being afield with an old friend—the old friend with whom I plinked my first tin can over forty years ago when I was still too young to be in school.

The dogs were content to let me break trail and, as I moved farther along, I was disappointed there was no fresh sign. It was impossible to know when the snow had come down but I suspected it had been in the last few hours, in which case, it would have covered sign made in the early evening and most of the night. The trail wound through aspen whips in a cutting that was about ten years old. I crossed one set of rabbit tracks that were from the last twelve hours but they were full of snow. When I was about ten yards past them I turned to check on the dogs and was surprised to see Starr had left my tracks to follow these old rabbit tracks. As she pushed through the snow, the top of her back was actually lower than the level of the snow. Nevertheless, she obviously had scent, and as she entered a snow-covered blowdown, I saw a rabbit bolt out the far side. It was bouncing along pretty well, but I probably could have snapped a shot or two had I wanted to. I was more interested in letting the dogs have a run. About the time the bunny passed out of sight, Starr opened up on the trail with her distinctive bawl.

Toby had passed me on the trail and now perked up his ears and looked into the brush where Starr was floundering along the track. Instead of "barking in" as he should have done (joining the chase), Toby watched and followed the chase by moving along parallel to it on the relatively hard packed trail. He was taking the easy way out and letting Starr do the work. Well, I had not expected real top-notch dog work. I was pleased however with the intensity Starr was showing on the trail. She was headed west, away from me and was trailing steadily. I lost sight of Toby and waited for him to chime in but that didn't happen.

Snow clung to the trees. The snow on the ground was soft and fluffy. A rabbit would be hard to spot in any cover, especially so if it ran one of the many previously packed trails. The packed trails were like troughs in the snow, and the bunny would be, in effect, running in a trench. While I was not really too concerned about killing rabbits for myself, I immediately wished I had opted for a shotgun. If I got shooting, it was likely to be snap shooting at a running target, and I really wanted to kill one in front of the dogs for their sake, especially Starr's.

The snowy landscape absorbed sound efficiently, and before long, the chase was sounding very faint. I knew the rabbit was not that far away, but hoped it would swing 'round soon. The dogs would have a terrible time with the snow, which meant the rabbit would not be pushed hard. In that situation, the rabbit often lets the dogs get very near to it and then puts on a run for a hundred yards or more, then sits back to relax a while. It can take a very long time for the customary circle route to be completed.

The light snow continued to fall, and there were songbirds active for a last feeding before the big storm. It was gray, mild and wintry. I could hear the county snowplow working the road and the snowmobiles starting up at the hunting shack a half-mile or so away. The fellows sounded excited to be at their shack snowmobiling with a big snow about to begin. I heard some whoops of excitement and then the roar of several machines starting off, headed towards the state trail just east of that shack. About then I heard the rabbit chase swing back in my direction.

It was all Starr so far. Not a peep from Toby, but the stocky little female had been yelping steadily the whole time, indicating she had been able to stay with the scent. It was hard to judge how close she was. It was also tricky in this situation because the rabbit might be ten feet or two hundred yards in front of the dog. I was in the "ready mode" that beaglers all know. Tense and watching for a sign of the rabbit, trying to stay quiet and to use a minimum of movement. It is easy to spook the rabbit, and you may not even see him when he spooks. There! A flash of movement. Yes, it was the rabbit, thirty yards distant and moving towards my rear over my left shoulder. I just saw a few bounces and it was into some balsam trees. I quietly turned to take a better position and watched the balsam patch intently. The rabbit may have stopped inside, may have run straight away, or really in any direction without me seeing it. It took several more minutes for Starr to come in sight. About the time she did, Toby showed up too, but Starr was on the track and Toby was still loafing and following the chase by moving along the packed trails.

Starr finally entered the balsams and I saw no rabbit come out the other side. As Starr moved through, I turned a bit to look in a different direction, towards where we had first jumped the hare, as the trail seemed to be heading for that area. No sooner had I turned than there it was, bouncing along the same trail it had followed when we initially jumped it. I got the gun to my shoulder and the hammer back but all I caught were glimpses of the fleeing critter. The dogs would have to bring it around again and I wished again for the shotgun, as both of these last sightings were such that I would have had a good chance with the scattergun.

Now Toby moved in and began to help on the trail. He didn't make any noise other than a little whimper. He was obviously the type who would only let loose with his voice when the scent was smoking hot. Starr on the other hand blabbered away with any bit of scent in her nose. They moved off in what seemed like an exact retracing of the rabbits initial escape route. In a few minutes, however, they lost the scent and the woods were still.

Well, they had run a complete circle and had given me a chance. That was a measure of success. The scent seemed to be holding well and the dogs seemed to want to hunt. So far so good. I moved towards the area where I had last heard Starr.

I was moving along trails that had been packed by earlier snowshoeing, so it was pleasant walking. Not like a city sidewalk to be sure, but not like breaking trail in unpacked snow, either. Toby showed up again and began to follow me. I heard a couple of tentative yelps from Starr but she had obviously been fooled now, and every minute she was off the scent the colder it would get. I hoped my moving around would perhaps move a rabbit or two and the dogs would pick them up. It was obvious by the absence of tracks that the rabbits were not moving on their own.

I moved across the ditch that meanders through the place and noticed fresh rabbit tracks that followed right along the frozen watercourse. Toby was now off ahead of me, but with a bit of coaxing I got him to come over and investigate the tracks. He immediately began to follow them but did not bark. I moved along the trail, keeping him in sight, waiting for the rabbit to jump or for Toby to open up, but neither event occurred, although it was obvious he had scent. Eventually he gave up and rejoined me. We moved out to the main trail and I sort of just lollygagged along hoping Starr would find game. Eventually she did and now Toby immediately ran to her to give her a hand. Things started to heat up and I heard Toby give an occasional bay as Starr sang away on the scent trail. As they moved off, I headed towards them, knowing there was a certain spot nearby that had always been an excellent rabbit crossing. I came up on the dogs as they tried to unravel the scent inside a small but thick stand of young balsam. Near this was a brush pile that was deeply covered with snow, thus forming a little knoll. I snowshoed up to the top of this and--using the snowshoes—packed an area down so that I might easily turn about. I decided that here I would wait, and see what turned up.

The dogs again got good scent and headed off towards the north. I heard Toby only rarely and, just as she had all day, Starr made the noise. For five minutes they were either headed away from me, or staying out away from me. Finally they turned and the chase got louder. Again I was in the lookout mode. The chase sounded as though it was coming at me straight as an arrow but unfortunately from a direction where my visibility was the poorest, the direction of those thick young balsams. I continually glanced left, right, and then towards the dogs, as there was a narrow alley through those balsams reaching about twenty-five yards out. It was about five feet wide. The dogs were now so close that it was certain the rabbit would pass, or perhaps already had passed, within twenty yards. The only question was whether I would get a shot or even see him.

My eyes swept back and forth and then suddenly there he was. Not zipping along or even hopping along. He was stopped at the far end of that open alley in the balsam! There were some branches across his body but there was no time to do anything but raise the gun and take a briefly aimed shot. At the crack of the little .22, the rabbit shuddered and sort of flattened out. As I worked the slide, he began running almost straight at me and then stopped twenty feet away behind a six-inch aspen. I leaned to the right and could see just a bit of him and shot again, missing and sending him scurrying into the balsam. It was obvious he was bit hard and I was sure he was mine. I moved off my little knoll and circled 'round the brush towards where I thought I would find either the rabbit or his trail. There he was, badly disabled but still alive, so I shot again to end the episode. We had a rabbit.

The hounds trailed to where I had shot him the first time and then seemed to lose the trail. I hung the bunny in a tree and took some photos. Toby showed up and posed as well. I called for Starr, knowing she would only come to me if it suited her, but thought perhaps she was looking for me. A shout would help her find me. I was flattering myself, I guess.

Toby and I made a circuit of the property hoping to find tracks or jump something. I did not hear Starr and suspected she may have headed for home. We found nothing of promise so headed back to the house. When I got there, Toby could not get inside fast enough. When he got in, he ran to the bedroom and leaped into the sack. Sherilee said Starr had scratched at the door at 8:30 and when the door was opened, she too had gone straight to the bed and straight to sleep. I guess they figured they had done enough for me for the day.

The snow was still light. I got the mail and filled the bird feeders. I joined my bride for coffee. It had been a fine morning. The dogs did well enough. I did well enough. They stuck with a tough line and I made a reasonably tough shot. We did not kill a lot, the dogs did not do anything amazing and I made no incredible shots. It was just a sort of so-so hunt. Most hunts are of that kind, and that is plenty for me. There will be many more hunts, I hope. Some will be "skunks" and some will be incredible but most will be just so-so like today was. Nevertheless, one hard-won rabbit, taken fairly, is still great fun.

I actually drove in to the office late that morning and worked for a couple of hours. When I got home, Sherilee said the beagles had gone back out right after I left, about 11:00 A.M. At about three, Toby was at the door and at dusk, about 5:45, Starr showed up. Toby was tired and Starr was so exhausted and stiff it took her three tries to jump up on the couch. Evidently, my beagles prefer to do their rabbit hunting without me. Perhaps they like the chase only and do not want me shooting their rabbits. Whatever. I had had a good hunt and a good day. I think they did, too.

It's 8:00 P.M. now, the end of the day of this hunt. Toby is sprawled on the family room floor and Starr has retreated to some dark corner of the house (most likely the spare bedroom in the basement) where she can rest without us bothering her. Officially, there are four more days of rabbit season, but I am sure that for me it is over for this year. As I write these words the snowflakes are still coming down, a little thicker now and the snow continues to pile up on the deck. Round two of the storm is supposed to be here tonight and perhaps another foot of snow by tomorrow night. There is something endearing about being at home on a weekend, safe and warm, waiting for or waiting out a snowstorm.

I will be on the roof tomorrow, shoveling off the winter's accumulation. I hauled several dozen duck decoys in from the garage this afternoon. They need to be cleaned up and repainted. It is truly the off-season now, the best time for touching up decoys and for taking care of miscellaneous items that need doing. The best time for remembering past hunts and for writing stories.

Jake and Jill

My golden retriever, Jill, turned six last December. She is my first bird dog, though I have had dogs nearly continuously throughout my life, including the beagles for rabbit hunting. She is the dog with which I first experienced the joy of very close teamwork between man and dog. Beagles do not rely on hand signals or any other help from their masters to do their job. The hunter brings them to the chosen area and turns them loose. The dog is then on its own. He finds the rabbit and then follows its scent for as long as it is able. The hunter does his best to get a shot. A bird dog, however, is expected to work close to its master while finding the game, taking signals from the hunter who uses hand, voice, whistle—or all three—to guide the dog. The dog is expected to be steady to wing and shot, and to retrieve on command. In the duck blind, he is to behave himself and wait patiently until there is game to retrieve, and then perform the retrieve on command, sometimes with directional commands from the hunter. Both dogs rely on their nose, ability and endurance. Beagles are full of heart and determination. I sometimes get the chills watching them work. The retriever's ability to work with its master is a thing of beauty. Each of the two breeds performs exactly as man has shaped them to.

Jill is my first attempt to develop the teamwork concept. She has an incredible nose and desire to match. Her preference is upland bird work, and she does a good job with grouse, pheasant and woodcock, though she would rather not retrieve a woodcock. Her waterfowl work is good and she has amazed me with some of her retrieves. There are faults in her work, to be sure, but she is not one of those half-trained dogs that cost you as many birds as they get for you. Overall, though, we have done well together, for I had never trained a dog to such a degree. She is a wonderful pet and housedog as well. She turned my wife from a woman who liked dogs to a woman who loves them. She came to us as a seven-week old pup in January 1996. My resident Alpha Female made it clear the pup could live in the house only until the weather moderated, and then would move outside with the beagles. Come spring, the beagles moved into the house to join Jill and the rest of us.

Jill's muzzle is getting white now, as is my own beard, and with her coat color not much different from my own hair color,

some people are beginning to say we look alike. That suits me fine, for people always comment what a pretty dog she is.

When I picked Jill, I was looking for the runt of the litter from a smallish sire and dam. Having never trained a waterfowl dog before, I was not sure if my training skills would result in a well-behaved dog. I do much of my hunting from a canoe. I reasoned if I had a dog that wasn't calm in the boat, I would rather have fifty pounds of moving ballast than eighty-five or ninety. I also thought I had a better chance of controlling a golden than a lab, though I had no real experience with either. My fears about a lack of control were for naught, for she is well behaved. Her diminutive stature, though, has been a handicap in the environment where I do most of my duck hunting. Most of her retrieves are in flooded tussock sedge and willow brush, and she has difficulty moving through it. This is not a huge problem when the duck comes down dead, but cripples can turn a sprint into a marathon. She is persistent and has pulled many a cripple out of that mess, some after a chase of as long as forty minutes. She is about all in when she returns, but most often, she has a bird in her mouth.

At six years old, I realize she will begin to lose some of her physical abilities soon. After having a dog like this for six seasons, I hope never to be without one. These dogs seem to hit their prime at about four years old. I have read this and heard it from more experienced dog handlers than me. Jill was that way. I thought the time was now right to acquire a pup and begin its training. If the dog progressed as well as Jill did in her first year, it would be doing some work already this fall. As Jill begins to slow down, the younger dog will hopefully be coming into its own. I decided to try another golden, but this time to go with a male for a bit more aggressiveness and size. I looked for a litter from a larger sire and dam. It only took a few days to locate a prospect.

We met Jake during the first week of February. The litter had eight pups, five of them males. All were very blonde and all of them looked large. The dam was about the same weight as Jill, longer but slimmer. The sire was a magnificent looking dog of ninety pounds. He was built like a bull, with very small hindquarters, a deep powerful chest, bull neck and a nice square head. I could hardly take my eyes off him—I had never seen a more beautiful golden retriever.

We handled all of the males and three of them seemed to be about the same size, just a little larger than their brothers and sisters, save one little gal who was noticeably smaller than her littermates. One of these bigger males chewed on me pretty hard. None seemed overly timid or overly aggressive. We picked what seemed like the biggest one and he seemed to have the squarest head, though that was hard to determine. We named him Floodwood River Jake, to go with Floodwood River Jill, his new mentor.

We went to visit him one more time before he was ready to leave his mom, and I picked him up and brought him home on February 15. As I drove through Duluth, he climbed on my lap, put his front paws against the door window and looked out at the lights of the city, calm as could be. When he got to the house, he investigated Jill and Starr as calmly as they investigated him. He walked over to Jill's sleeping pad and plunked himself down for a nap. No whining and no signs of any distress. It was as if he had lived here for years.

For some of us, the excitement of picking out and picking up a new puppy does not diminish with time. Just like when I was a kid, I held the little fur ball a lot, played with him and let him chew on my hands. We were impressed with his calm demeanor, which hasn't changed a bit so far. He does get playful a lot, but never out of control, and he seems to adapt well to new situations.

Jill is a dog that needs attention. When "guest dogs" or little kids are around, she sometimes gets in what appears to be a little huff. She isn't surly or anything, she just ambles off to a quiet corner. It's as if she is telling anyone who might be watching that she knows she won't be the center of attention for a while. When we come to our senses and are ready to show her proper affection and attention, she will be available. She tried hard to "not like" Jake. She would turn away from him when he came to pull on her ears and play, or try to pretend he wasn't there at all. That was hard a lot of the time, because the pup would just barrel into her, throw his hindquarters against her and drop his chin down on the floor to invite her to play. Before long, she gave a begrudging chew on his ear, then a paw on his back. Within a week or so of his arrival, Jill dropped the charade and just dove into being his playmate.

Jake began his basic training at nine weeks old. He was a little more headstrong than Jill had been when she started, but he learned quickly what was expected of him. He just had a little more trouble going along with it than Jill had. He quickly mastered "sit" and "stay." He began chasing dummies but not bringing them to hand. Before long he was all legs and feet and quite clumsy. Those paws seemed to double in size every few days. The months to come would reveal a lot about little Jake as a hunting dog. It was obvious from the start that he was a great companion.

Habitat Work

In the extreme northwest corner of our property, there was a very thick and wet alder swamp. When I first made a cross-country ski trail near it, my wife followed it alone one day. When she got back to the house, she said this swamp looked spooky. Like bear country. That is how Bear Country Pond, which is right adjacent to and "upstream" of this swamp, got its name. My brother-in-law, Tim, sarcastically called the swamp "God's Country" after drawing the short straw for a deer drive and having to cross this piece of ground. I had eyed up this swamp for years, wondering how I might improve it. The plan I came up with was a bit grand, by my standards, but workable. I thought I could build a dike that followed the property line. I would flood the entire corner. I would first shear the brush off the site so that when it was flooded it would be free of most of that brush. My plan was hatched, fine-tuned, and submitted to the DNR and other groups for review in hopes they would like it enough to kick loose some of their cash to help with it. The DNR came through and I found myself a contractor.

In February the work began. A D7 Caterpillar with a shear blade on its front sliced off the brush in three hours time. With this specially designed blade and frozen ground, the power of the big machine allowed the operator to run at a high speed. The dozer left to do shearing work on other sites after this phase was completed. Then the blade was changed to the normal type, and it was back a week later to begin excavating. A trench was dug around the entire perimeter of the area, the dirt piled and rough leveled where the dike would be. That was all we could do during the winter. The fine leveling of the dirt and placement of water level control devices would have to wait for dry summer weather.

When I have such a project underway, I like to visit it often, even if there is no work going on. Most weekends I would walk out to the "new pond" and look it over. I would pick spots where I thought wild rice would do best, or arrowhead would do best, or where a duck blind or observation blind would work well. I wondered how the deer travel patterns would change when the area was flooded. I intentionally had the dozer operator leave many large ash trees standing. They would likely die when the water level went up, but this would give the pond a bit more the appearance of a natural beaver pond. Blue herons like to establish nesting colonies in such places. One such rookery, just east of my home, had been recently abandoned. The beaver colony was trapped out and the dams destroyed. This beautiful series of beaver ponds had created that heron rookery when the flooding killed the ash trees. The dead, flooded timber had been a major roost for wood ducks. I heard the county highway department had wanted the dams out of there because they had raised the water level in the roadside ditches upstream. I hope that is not the case, for many of us in the neighborhood have spent much time, money, and sweat to create wetland areas. The destruction of those dams destroyed more wetland than my neighbors and I will ever be able to create.

Besides walking this new pond area, I often sat and tried to envision what it would be like when the entire area was covered with a sheet of water. There would be wild rice and arrowhead plants waving in the breeze, and groups of ducklings following their mother in and out of the cattails. With luck, by summer's end, I would not need to use my imagination to see at least some of this.

The alterations, large or small, that man makes to the landscape will affect our wild neighbors. My home stands on ground that had once been cloaked in virgin pine. The loggers had con-

verted the pine to an unsightly slash pile, and a new group of wild occupants moved in to replace the species that needed the pine forest. The slashing soon was covered with brush, then second-growth forest. The homesteader who first lived on the property probably cut it to use as firewood, and perhaps he logged a little of that second growth forest to supplement his income. Each time the landscape changed, a new group of birds and animals moved in to use it, and each time, another community of wild creatures became homeless. Some would be mobile enough and lucky enough to find suitable habitat in another location, many would not. Finding that habitat is only the first step, for it may well be inhabited and defended by others of their kind.

Eventually, a farmer needed more field land and cleared some of the trees. Again a shift occurred. Finally, I built a home in one of the hay fields, created a yard and planted pine trees around it. The red squirrels are again feasting on the seeds of Norway pine here, for the first time in perhaps seventy-five years.

In my wanderings on our seventy-seven acres, I am always looking at changes I might make to benefit one type of wildlife or another. While I attempt to create a diverse landscape that will support diverse wildlife, I show my preference for waterfowl by devoting most of my time, money and energy to creating ponds and wetlands. There is great satisfaction in knowing that ducklings, perhaps a hundred or more each year, will be produced in and around my ponds. Places where, for centuries, no duckling had existed. In addition to providing me with entertaining viewing, they will more than replace the ducks I kill each year.

Other game species get special treatment as well, but so do the bluebirds and the tree swallows that now enjoy thirty or more additional nesting places that were built and positioned with them in mind. Another hundred or so of these birds are produced each year on the property.

One of the first projects undertaken after we purchased the land was to cut down a decadent stand of alder. It was perhaps one-eighth of an acre in size. The mostly dead or dying trees were cut down and piled. The next spring and summer, increased sunlight on the forest floor created a green carpet of succulent plants that deer, rabbits and grouse eagerly fed on. The rabbits and chipmunks took shelter in the piled brush, as did songbirds. The brush piles soon became overgrown with raspberry bushes. Eventually, the alder sprouts again began to shade the ground. Now, their close growing stalks make excellent cover for woodcock. Watching the succession of plants and animals on this and other projects is a learning experience that a classroom will never equal.

When your visions turn into reality, and the wildlife responds in the way you had hoped, it is difficult to describe the satisfaction you feel. With each walk I take, I will dream and plan some more. I will admire what has already been accomplished. Not for what it has brought me, though that is much appreciated. The feelings go far beyond that. Good things have been accomplished, and to be a part of that is its own reward.

Varmints

I was probably about fourteen when I ordered the catalog from Burnham Brothers, one of the companies that was a pioneer in the manufacture of predator calls. The idea of calling in a fox, coyote or bobcat seemed exciting. In those days, many of the catalogs of outdoor gear included pictures and even stories of hunters and sportsmen using that gear. As I recall, the Burnham Brothers catalog included a little history of how these boys got into varmint calling. I know the book was filled with photos of the two men standing over dead coyotes, fox, and bobcat set up in a line that seemed to stretch awfully wide. I ordered the long-range call.

When I got my new toy in the mail, I read the instructions and tried varmint hunting for the first time. It was a bust. I tried it a few more times while I was in high school and managed to call in some crows once. During that stage of my hunting career, I did not have a whole lot of patience. I could go out repeatedly to hunt deer because I got a glimpse of deer regularly and everyone talked about deer hunting. That kept my enthusiasm up. However, I did not have the patience to learn predator calling. In my normal travels in the woods, I saw fox now and again, and I killed a coyote more or less accidentally one year while deer hunting. But I just couldn't stay fired up enough to stick with hunting critters that seemed more like ghosts than like real animals. In the years since then, I have occasionally tried varmint calling but with no more success than what I had in those first years. It was something to do in the off months when there was little or nothing else to hunt. Even today I often carry a squealer call when I bow hunt, just on the off chance I see a coyote or fox, thinking I might be able to call it in for a shot.

I know very little about this business of predator calling. I have called ducks and geese with some success, but the squealing rabbit routine is still pretty much like voodoo as far as I am concerned. However, these days my kids are all grown up and have moved away, and they have jobs. They apparently still love me, or at least put on the appearance of doing so. Each Christmas now, I end up with some mighty fine hardware, courtesy of my offspring. They even listen to my hints. Christmas before last, I suggested one of those electronic calling devices might be appreciated and would likely get some use. Besides being legal for predators, they may be used for crows and even snow geese during the spring conservation seasons. Then, on Christmas, what to my wondering eyes did appear... but the said electronic caller.

I just had to try out one tape that came along with the kit. It was called "coyote serenade." It was an immediate hit with the dogs in the house, who all came running hell-bent to my new toy—and me—barking, growling and then howling in chorus with the recorded sounds of their wild brethren. I thought to myself, "Is it real or is it Memorex?"

I couldn't wait to try this gizmo out on the local varmints. I made one trip by myself with no success, then another with two pals who knew even less about varmint hunting than I did, but who were anxious to get out and hunt for something. There was a considerable amount of snow on the ground at the time, so Rod, Jeff and I donned our snowshoes and hoofed it into the woods one Saturday morning. Jeff is a real comic. When the pitiful sounds of the dying rabbit tape started the first time, he looked at me and made his lower lip quiver as if he was going to cry. We set up two or three times that day in different locations and let the rabbit squealing tape run through. I sat by the caller with my shotgun and turkey loads. Rod and Jeff watched from distant vantage points with their .223 rifles. No varmints. However, it was good exercise and we didn't have to dish out any cash to a fitness center.

I used my new secret weapon a little for crow hunting that first spring, but not much. It did not sound as good as the homemade unit my son-in-law rigged up in my garage using an old car stereo and plastic battery case.

This winter, I gave it another try. My brother-in-law, Wes, and I got together one chilly Saturday morning and walked out at sunrise to the south end of my property. It was a gray morning, with a breeze. The ground was snow covered but not to any depth that would make it rough going. We set up in a little blind made of cedar posts near my south property line. We put out the caller, got into the blind, and set up to watch different directions. I hit the switch on the caller. When the pitiful wail of the expiring rabbit cut the morning stillness, Wes turned to me and winced.

"This is why girls don't varmint hunt," I whispered to him.

We called from this location for about twenty minutes, and then moved a quarter-mile and did another twenty-minute sequence. Nothing doing at either place, but we saw some coyote tracks that looked fresh and thought perhaps one of the critters had at least been investigating our call. We set up once more and had the same results, then headed back to the house for coffee. I suppose this was about the tenth or twelfth time I had actually gone varmint hunting, and each time the result was about the same. I just did not have the voodoo magic that is required.

Never one to give up easily, I tried again a week or so later, this time with my neighbor Rex. It was another cool and gray morning, and we did exactly the same routine that Wes and I had tried on the previous hunt. We left at dawn and sat in the same three spots for about the same length of time. At the third location, I set up on the ground, sitting down and leaning my back against an ash tree. I was on the edge of the new pond site, where the brush had recently been cleared. Rex took a stand atop one of the big brush piles the dozer operator had made on the edge of the pond site. We started the caller and began the routine of waiting, yet again. I did not have much confidence, as you can imagine. My mind wandered and I started to think about other things I needed to do that day. I wished it were spring. Some crows were passing by, very high and a long way off. I wished they would swing close enough to let me try a shot.

Pow! A shot rang out and shook me out of my daydream. I looked over at Rex and he was staring at an area behind me and over my right shoulder. I got up and looked around, seeing nothing. I walked out into the open and looked for a carcass or a running animal but neither could be seen. Rex climbed down from his perch and walked over.

"What was it?" I asked.

"Fox!" he replied.

We walked towards my back field as he explained what had happened.

Rex had been in the same daze as I after two setups with no action. He was shaken from his trance by the appearance of a fox, standing in the middle of the cleared area and about a hundred yards in front of him (to the west). He brought up his gun and trained the scope on the fox. Just as he was getting on target, it ran off in a southerly direction. He thought it had been spooked off, but it stopped again and gave him another chance to get his sights on it. However, just at the last second, it took off on the run again and into the woods on the south side of the cleared area. I was sitting directly south of Rex and facing him, so the fox was now to my left and a little behind me. Of course, I was asleep with open eyes at the time, and clueless. The wary animal now moved in an easterly direction, obviously to get down wind of the calls he was hearing, the wind being north-northwest. When it got downwind of me it appeared to catch my scent and ran southeast into an opening, following the edge of one of the ponds. It was easily two hundred yards from Rex and trotting when he finally took his shot.

We found the critter's tracks on the crusty snow and there was no sign of a hit. As usual, after a shooting incident in the field, we talked excitedly about all that had happened, how we might have done it differently, and how we would do it the next time in hopes of a better outcome. Obviously, it would have worked well—in this case—to have one gunner downwind of the caller.

So finally, we had a measure of success with a varmint call. I hadn't even seen the animal but my partner had, and I consider it a small victory. I will be out there again, trying to lure in one of these wary predators. I hope it's not another thirty years before our next sighting!

March

The old saying describes March arriving as a lion and leaving like a lamb. Here in northeast Minnesota, the lion and lamb often come and go several times throughout the month. Nearly every month of the year has a distinctive flavor for me. When I think of July or October or most of the other months, specific weather and wildlife activity quickly come to mind. With March, I had to stop and think; I even consulted my journals to review several years' worth of entries recorded during the month. Having done so, it is obvious why March had no distinctive trademarks. Mother Nature cannot seem to make up her mind in March, and the extreme variability of conditions will mask one's "definition" of the month.

The journal entries are filled with notes about late winter storms as well as beautiful spring-like weather. A few years, the first wood ducks and geese have appeared in March. In other years the streams and bodies of water are tightly locked in ice well beyond the last days of this page of the calendar. One March, we found our first wood tick of the year on the 14th and we have located nests of saw-whet and great horned owls—with eggs in them—during this, the third month of the year. By month's end we usually have plenty of days that tease us into thinking spring might actually be here or at least that it is just around the corner. Likewise, we will usually have days when it seems we are in the midst of winter. March weather is definitely a mixed bag.

In 2002, we got our first sustained cold snap of the winter and were reminded about twenty below zero mornings and what wind chill values mean. Before we fully recovered from that unpleasant slap in the face, we got back-to-back snowstorms that gave us eighteen inches of snow or more. The snow banks alongside the road were higher than they had been at any time during the winter. My plans for a leisurely ride around the property to maintain my wood duck boxes were dashed by these snowstorms. The snow was now too deep for the four-wheeler to handle. The weather stayed cold through the entire month.

March is a slow time of year for the hunter, but not for the true outdoorsman. The life of a hunter is wonderful. That of an outdoorsman is even better.

Ducks in the Living Room

My three-year old grandson, Connor, loves to watch movies. When he stays with us he usually asks to watch one of the many kid's movies we have on tape. One Friday night, when he arrived for a weekend visit, he asked to watch a movie, just as he always does. I asked if he wanted to watch a duck-hunting movie, and he replied that he did. So, down to the family room we went. I dug out one of my many duck hunting videos. I popped it in the VCR and expected to watch about five minutes of it before he grew bored. Much to my pleasant surprise, the young man could not take his eyes off the duck hunt!

Later that evening, he explored the house with me for the thousandth time of his young life. In my den, he had a new interest in the duck calls that hung from their lanyards on a nail in the wall, as well as my closet full of camo clothes.

"Les pway dunk hunting, Bapa," he said. (Let's play duck hunting, Grandpa.) So, we suited up and got our calls around our necks. We set up some decoys in the family room, played the video again and shot ducks until it was time for bed. The next morning, Connor and I were the first ones up, as usual. The morning is our quality time together, for we two rise earlier than the rest of the family. Right after breakfast, my new duck-hunting partner asked if we could "pway dunk hunting" again. Of course, we did.

Connor has been back to visit two or three times since our

first "dunk hunt," and each time, he has asked to go on another hunt. We have fine-tuned our approach. We sometimes hunt from the boat (our couch) and sometimes from a blind made of a coffee table and some couch pillows. I am pleased that during our last hunt, Connor didn't just toot on the call, but tried to mimic the callers on the video. He can't come close on the actual sounds, but he is getting very close on the rhythm and tempo. He is also mimicking the phrases he hears the hunters say and does the high five with me when a duck splashes down.

We watch the video and when ducks are coming in, the conversation goes something like this.

"Get ready Connor, here they come."
"I weddy."
"OK, take 'em!"

We shoot our imaginary shotguns and a duck splashes down.
"I got him Connor!"
"NO BAPA I GOTST HIM."
"CLAIMER!"
"No Bapa… YOU claimer."

I have high hopes for this lad.

Farewell to a Friend

On the last weekend of March, my family said goodbye to a good friend. Toby, our beagle, was killed by a car in front of my daughter's home. He was ten years old and had moved in with Tara and Derek last summer when they bought their country home. Tara has always loved animals. Derek had never had a dog. When the kids got their new place, Toby "retired" to live with them. A golden retriever pup and two cats joined him. He had a nice place there for his short retirement, with both human and animal companionship. It is hard to lose him for he was quite the dog.

Toby was not the hard hunting beagle that many of my other hounds had been. He ran rabbits, but by the time he joined us I was not rabbit hunting the way I had years before. I got him started, but didn't follow through with many hours afield hunting over him. He did a passable job, but never became the sort of hound that went crazy at the sight of a gun and tore off to find a rabbit. This was all due to me not hunting over him much. He hunted for himself because it was fun, not as part of a team. Not that we didn't kill a few bunnies together, but as I said, we didn't go after them as I had in the years before. Our other beagle, Starr, and Toby, hunted together a lot on their own. Often, they would be gone overnight, and the sound of their hound music could be heard as they happily persecuted the snowshoe hare in our neighborhood. In fact, these two didn't much care to hunt with anyone else but each other. If I went out with them, they seemed to prefer following me around over beating the brush for fresh scent. Then, after we got home from such an outing, they would head off together without me, going after those bunnies like gangbusters. As if to say, "Who needs that guy?" After Toby moved to Elk River, neither dog showed any interest in hunting—except when Toby came home to Cedar Valley. When that happened, they often were on hot rabbit scent within minutes of Toby jumping out of Tara's car. Toby and Starr were unique among my dogs in that they did not see me as their favorite hunting partner. I learned to deal with it.

Toby lived a life filled with adventure and narrow escapes. Over the years, he was lost as a young pup, later found—miles from our house—and returned by a neighbor. He was hit by a car, caught in a coyote snare for two days, and on two occasions, badly mauled by wild critters. Each of these scrapes nearly killed him. Each time he recovered after a week or so of sleeping and rest. Usually, he slept round the clock right after such an episode. He was tough as nails. After the first car hit, for a time he couldn't move his neck properly. He walked around with his chin sort of tucked in. When he walked up to you, he couldn't bend his neck to point his nose towards you. To look at you, he just rolled his eyes and it looked hilarious. During his last year, one of his legs didn't move correctly. Backward motion wasn't a problem, but as he took a step and brought the leg forward, he had to swing it out away from his body in a wide arc. He had also been having seizures for about two years. Still, he was a gentle dog that loved people, even the little kids who pestered him when he was stiff and sore and in need of a nap. Some days he acted like a puppy and played with the other dogs, racing around at top speed and barking. All of his life, and especially when he was young, you might see him trotting across the yard, then just suddenly dropping down and rolling over a few times and then popping back up and resuming his trot. To us it seemed like something he did just because he was in a good mood, like a person might jump up and kick their heels together just because they were in good spirits. Our sons thought Toby was the best of any of our dogs.

The day Toby died, we had just left Tara and Derek's and gone to our son Ben's place. It was Easter weekend and we had planned a nice day with our kids for Saturday. Of course, the accident put quite a damper on this. Tara was especially devastated. I felt the hurt myself, but I had to help Tara. My own feelings were buried a little. On Easter Sunday, we went to church and then drove home. That morning, I was awake before anyone else and thoughts of my pal Toby filled my mind. When we got home I sat down and wrote a little piece about the wonderful friend, who was now gone.

Cedar Valley Toby, AKA Toby, or "The Tobster," went on his last hunt on March 30th, 2002. We were at Tara and Derek's and had brought Starr and the retrievers down with us. Toby and Starr had gotten to where they would only go hunting when they were together, and with Toby in Elk River and Starr in Cedar Valley, that hadn't happened often in the last year. But every time Toby came home to CV, he and Starr were off to the swamps right away to run rabbits. Yesterday they apparently tried it in Elk River and Toby was hit, and killed, by a car. The fun weekend we had planned for Easter in the cities was dampened quite a lot. Toby was ten. I almost said he had ten good years, but if you know his story, you know he had his share of bad days, if not bad years. Twice mauled by wild critters, caught in a snare for two days and hit by a car a couple of years ago. He always bounced back. Though he had gotten sore and stiff and was having occasional seizures, I had gotten to seeing him as indestructible. I find it hard to believe there was a car built that could take out the Tobster. The car is likely totaled. Or maybe, it is made of green Kryptonite. I remember asking my mom when I was little if dogs went to heaven and she explained that animals do not have a soul, so they don't go to heaven. But if they did, we can imagine what dog heaven would be like. First of all, there would probably not be any cats there, or if there were, they wouldn't have claws. Angel dogs would be able to climb trees and the trees there would be full of squirrels and raccoons. There would be cedar and alder swamps full of slow stupid rabbits. There would be ponds full of one winged ducks and a lot of the grouse and pheasants would not be able to fly. There would be warm, sunny places and cool, shady places to lie down. Bedroom slippers and shoes would grow from low bushes where they would be easy to reach. There would be people there, of course, because just as people need dogs, dogs need people. These people would have pockets full of dog treats and would always want to throw sticks or a ball or scratch the Angel dogs wherever they needed to be scratched. In dog heaven, the Angel dogs would be allowed to chase deer and if the people chased deer, the dogs would be allowed to shoot the people if they wanted to. But dogs are never vengeful even on earth, so they wouldn't. There would be a fire hydrant behind every tree. There would be a couple of roads running through dog heaven, too. Whenever the dogs wanted to, they could just put one paw on the edge of the road and a pickup truck would stop. The dog could jump into the box or into the cab to ride as long as they felt like it, with their head out the window and their tongue flapping in the breeze. They could chase cars on the road and if they caught one, it would turn into a hamburger. If one of the cars happened to hit a dog, the car would roll over into the ditch and die. There are small tipsy garbage cans all over dog heaven and they are full of steaks. (Listen up Starr!) Best of all, everywhere you look in dog heaven there are dead smelly animals to roll in.

This is all kind of silly, but I am mourning my buddy, Toby, so you need to humor me. I am gonna miss him. He loved people but was a dog's dog.

When I finished writing, I read it to Sherilee. We both laughed. We laughed so hard that we cried. Then we just cried.

April

April is the month when spring arrives. It might not be very spring-like at times, but in April, winter is only making its last gasp to let you know it will be back. Winter is stubborn, but in April, it is outgunned and on its way out of our neighborhood. In 2002, winter gave up the ghost more grudgingly than usual.

Each April the birds return. Not all, but legions of them will appear. In April, my journal entries are filled with the first annual sightings of many kinds of birds, especially the waterfowl, for I look for them in particular and make a point of recording their appearance. The teal may not show up in April, but the Canada Geese, mallards, wood ducks and hooded mergansers will be here.

It is impossible to describe April wildlife activity in a short summary. Migration, abandonment of winter dens, courting and breeding—all will begin and gradually turn into the frenzied activity of spring. From April through June, the wild community has more going on than at any other time of year. I walk the property often, watching the ice disappear and waiting for our first ducks to arrive. Some of the new sounds I hear each April are the drumming of the grouse and the drumming of the woodpeckers. In 2002, it seemed there were fewer drummers among both species. In recent years, I have listened closely for the crowing of a cock pheasant. I hope to learn that some of the birds I release each year have survived. At times, I have heard three or more, crowing from distinct locations. In 2002, I heard no crowing.

There may be last minute repairs to do on the duck boxes and nest structures, for the wood ducks and hooded mergansers will come looking for homes by month's end. Then it is time to watch, and to wait.

The Banquet

The town I refer to as my hometown is Floodwood, Minnesota. Its population is around 600. It is perhaps forty miles from Floodwood to any community that numbers over a thousand people. You might say it is almost remote. The surrounding countryside contains many farms, though active farms are quickly disappearing. There is a lot of wild, forested land around, or near the town. Logging and farming have been the staples of the economy here since the city came into being just over a hundred years ago. Naturally, this sort of rural community has a large percentage of its population active in the outdoor sports. It is also home to a small group of very dedicated sportsmen, whose love of the outdoors is matched by a love for their community. That affection extends to the wildlife resources with which our state is blessed. In the early 1980s, a group of these men became active in a group known as Geese Unlimited. GU is a drastically scaled down version of the well-known Ducks Unlimited organization. GU was formed with a primary goal of helping Canada goose populations expand in greater Minnesota.

Canada geese are one of those unusual species of wildlife that seem to thrive in close proximity to man. In fact, they have adapted extremely well to urban areas. City parks, golf courses and well-groomed lawns provide geese with food, for they are grazing birds. Cities with agricultural fields surrounding them, and with a supply of water, are like paradise to geese. This is especially true for the giant Canada goose subspecies. Two of Minnesota's urban areas, Rochester and the Minneapolis-St.Paul area, have ideal conditions for these giant birds. In the last twenty to thirty years, the population of giant Canada geese in these areas has exploded. Geese are beautiful birds and most of us can relate to the songs and stories about the haunting calls of wild geese. Twice each year, their calls proclaim to the world that the season is about to change. These birds mate for life and their families stay together longer than most bird families do. The parent birds are fearless in defense of their young. We tend to admire creatures that behave in ways resembling the human ideal of a moral lifestyle. It's hard to find someone who will say something bad about the Canada goose, if you are talking to people who have only seen them flying over in huge flocks each spring and autumn. However, once a pair, a family or a flock of them decides they like someone's yard, park or golf course, the goose can lose its charm quickly. Therefore, Minnesota's cities have grown decidedly anti-goose. Apparently, their citizens do not like to step in goose doo doo as they go about their daily business. Enter Geese Unlimited and the men from Floodwood.

Young geese usually imprint on the area where they learn to fly. It is that area the young goose will return to when it is mature enough to mate. Therefore, the geese that are born in the city and learn to fly there, eventually return there to raise babies of their own. Most cities do not allow hunting within their borders, and there are not many natural goose predators left roaming the streets of Minneapolis. The percentage of young geese that survive to breeding age is probably a lot greater for city-raised geese than it would be for geese hatched in the Canadian wilderness. You see where this is going. City geese have it made, and their numbers just keep increasing. How do you break, or at least slow down, this cycle? You can kill a lot of geese, but that generally doesn't go over well in a metropolitan area. It seemed as though the best idea for reducing this urban goose population was to round up the young geese before they learned to fly and move them somewhere far from the city. Then, when they did take wing, they would imprint on that area and not return to the city.

The State DNR and Geese Unlimited collaborated with the University of Minnesota to execute such a plan, beginning in about 1990. The U of M folks took care of the roundup chore, and the DNR, with GU assistance, moved birds to distribution sights in rural parts of the state. Interested individuals could request geese for release on sites where they, for whatever reason, wanted to have geese. The DNR reviewed the suitability of the planned release sights and had the final say as to whether the release would be permitted. The Floodwood members of GU were very active in actually moving the geese. The program was a great success in at least one respect. The transplanted geese did imprint on their release sites, or at least returned to areas near their release site, to nest. These birds would otherwise have returned to the urban areas. However, the urban populations of geese are still too large.

I have lived near Floodwood for thirty years. For most of that time, nesting geese were unheard of in my area. We saw the spring and fall movements of the birds, and occasionally we might see a flock resting on a local field or beaver pond. However, all that has changed dramatically in the last fifteen years. Breeding pairs are common on beaver ponds, lakes, and along the rivers that abound here. Now, in late summer, it is common to see geese gathering into larger and larger flocks, congregating on area fields or moving at low altitude between feeding and roosting areas. The beautiful giant Canada goose is now counted among the common species of breeding waterfowl in this area. A season or two ago—for the first time ever—Minnesota hunters harvested more Canada geese than they did mallards. No state in the nation harvests more of these big birds than Minnesota. The Geese Unlimited group played a large role in making this happen, and my neighbors from the Floodwood area played a major role in GU.

With their mission accomplished, the GU organization closed its doors and ceased to exist in 1999. However, my neighbors were not ready to stop working on behalf of their beloved waterfowl. In late 1999, the same core group who made Floodwood GU a success affiliated themselves with the Minnesota Waterfowl Association (MWA) as the Floodwood, Geese Unlimited Chapter. It was then that I hooked up with these fellows. I had been in touch with MWA, looking for help with a wetland project on my property. They informed me that the new chapter had just formed in Floodwood. I attended the next meeting. The MWA is yet another Ducks Unlimited type of organization. Their mission is to raise money within Minnesota, to help ducks in Minnesota. There were about eight men involved in the Floodwood chapter. There were more, of course, but about eight that made things go. I have tried to stay involved ever since. The biggest event of the year for the group is the annual banquet.

My family was well represented at the April 6 banquet, filling one table. About a hundred folks attended. The MWA Executive Director and the DNR Area Wildlife Manager talked about our organization and waterfowl management.

There were auctions, games, prizes and plenty of food. Wildlife art, guns and gear filled the banquet room. The twenty kids that attended were wide-eyed and hopeful as they checked out the prizes and games. We see to it that every kid goes home with at least one prize. Most go home with many more than that. It is a good banquet, and most of our guests have been attending for years. We have kept the attendance to one hundred and put an emphasis on the kids and a family atmosphere. This may not be wise if you are considering the bottom line, for kids don't spend as much as grownups do. However, the chapter is okay with making a little less money, if we can keep the evening a fun, family night out. The kids are the future of waterfowling, so we are planting a seed.

The banquet depends on the generosity of the business community, and that of the guests, for its success. Neither the guests nor the businesses let us down. Sportsmen and sportswomen open their wallets quickly for events like this. Yes, the guests have a chance to win something, but if you have done the banquet thing, you know that in the end, you are buying that gear at premium prices. When it's fun and for a good cause, it's not painful in the least.

My family came home with a big basket of prizes, including three guns. I have taken part in many banquets and always hoped for a gun, but this was the first time I came home with one. My son-in-law, Derek, came home with two! My table also provided some entertainment for the crowd as my daughter, Tara, and her uncle, got into a bidding war on a painting. Her uncle did the same with another friend at our table. A good time was had by all. Afterwards at home, we were up late, talking about the fun. The chapter did well on the fund raising.

On the morning after the banquet, I woke before the rest of the household. I took my cup of coffee and went out to the deck, wanting to check the weather. I was surprised the water puddles on the road had not frozen overnight, and even at that early hour, the snow was melting. It actually seemed as though it had warmed up during the night, and it was the most pleasant morning of the young spring. In the distance, I heard a honk. I turned to the west. A lone Canada goose winged into view, not very high. He (or she) gave a lonesome sounding honk as it passed over the yard. I wonder if the big bird was saying thank you.

The Return

In a recent check of my journal, I found that for several years running, the first waterfowl of the young spring visit my ponds during the first days of April. As these birds move north with the melting of the ice on major rivers, they seem to begin exploring the smaller bodies of water with urgency. They are looking for a place where they can begin the important task of feeding, to replace the spent reserves in their bodies. They must do so, and do so quickly, in order to have the strength and resources for reproduction. After the rivers open, the shallow ponds will thaw. The invertebrates in these become active and available for the hungry ducks. Mallards and Canada geese are the first to investigate the manmade ponds on our property, and then the hooded mergansers and wood ducks follow close on their heels. Blue-winged teal, the latest of the nesters that frequent our little wetlands, will be the last to show up. Except for the geese, all of those species are almost sure to nest in our little refuge each year. The geese frequent our ponds but have yet to nest there. Last year, two different pairs of these large birds were regulars on our property, and I was certain one pair was preparing to nest. Instead of taking wing when I got close to them, they lay their necks low and parallel to the water in an effort to hide, just as you might observe them doing when on or near a nest. I was disappointed when they quit the property after two weeks, without nesting. However, 2002 was another year, and I hoped it would be the year that a honker pair took up residence in our backyard refuge.

On April 9, for the first time in over twenty-eight years, I found myself unemployed. For years when talking with friends and coworkers about the job, I had joked that my worst fear about losing my job was it might happen when the hunting seasons had just closed. So in that respect, the timing pretty much fit the worst nightmare scenario. On the other hand, I would have plenty of time to observe the rites of spring in woodland, field and marsh. On April 10, I saw the first mallards of the season wing over the west-end of the property, looking for open water. There were only scattered areas where the runoff had melted away the ice. Geese had been in the area for several days. Our winter had been easy until March arrived, then we were treated to one of the coldest March's on record. In spite of an easy winter, spring arrived just a tad late.

On April 12, the day dawned with sunshine and frost. Even the somber earth tones of the winterkilled grass and leafless trees took on a cheerful look when the morning sun glinted off the frost crystals that clung to the bare branches and browned grass. A morning walk was definitely in order.

The drumming of a ruffed grouse came to me on the breeze from an area we had logged ten years earlier. Five deer fled when the two retrievers and I interrupted them from their feeding, in a sunny, open area. A robin or two flew overhead. The crows made the usual amount of morning racket that crows do. The honking of geese was almost constant, as pairs and small flocks moved to and fro in the sky. Several were obviously on my neighbor's property, just to the north of my place—the property he turned into a little paradise for geese. I spotted a woodcock on the shoulder of our driveway.

At Old Pond, the little sixty-foot by ninety-foot rectangular pond that was the first constructed on my place back in 1985, I jumped a mallard pair. Therefore, it was on the 12th that I officially recorded the first ducks "on property" for 2002. They took wing and cursed me.

I continued my walk and stopped to look at the large, muddy puddle that would soon be a four and one-quarter-acre pond and marsh. The mallard pair circled overhead and now cursed at a second pair, and was cursed by them in return. Later a trio of drakes passed over, circled and almost dropped into the new pond, but spotted little Jake romping on the bank and flared off. Three geese approached from the east and a pair from the west, all honking, and heading towards each other. As they came near each other, the pair set their wings and dropped down into the neighbor's property, joined by one of the trio. His two companions circled back once as if trying to convince him to stay in their company, then resumed their flight in the direction they had been headed. Then I heard the unmistakable squeal of a wood duck. The "Return" was underway.

That day the skim ice, covering most of the pools, would disappear by early afternoon. Ducks that were constantly on the move in search of those first open ponds would likely find these pools and pitch into them as soon as the ice gave way to open water. At least I reasoned so. An afternoon walk was in order to test my reasoning. In mid-afternoon, I walked the same route I had covered in the morning and jumped one pair each of wood ducks, hooded mergansers and mallards. The woodies were in Old Pond, and a hooded hen jumped up near the outlet of Bear Country Pond. She left with the characteristic grunting call that identifies the hooded merganser hen. I thought her to be alone, but perhaps five to ten seconds after she flushed, her mate surfaced less than forty feet from me. He had been submerged, searching for food, at the time his mate fled the scene. Years before, in this same pond at about the same time of year, I had watched a pair of hoodeds in courtship. The male, resplendent in his striking black and white crest, presented his ladylove with a fine, fat, wiggling minnow. She stood perched on the ice at the edge of open water and her suitor dove frequently until finally he surfaced with the minnow, hopped up on the ice next to his hen and laid the prize before her. She promptly walked over to open water, hopped in, and began diving for a minnow of her own. The male I saw on April 12, 2002 looked very perplexed when he surfaced and found his mate had disappeared. Then he saw me and immediately flushed. A mallard pair I hadn't seen flushed from the other side of the pond. As they did, I spotted a pair of geese, one standing and one sitting, on the far side of the pond and across the dike that surrounded it. I began to walk around the pond to get closer, and they lay their necks down so their chins were almost touching the water.

As the dogs and I got closer, the geese walked further out on the ice shelf then swam off just a little way. I sat down to watch them from about sixty feet distant. They showed only caution and no real alarm. Jill, the veteran waterfowl dog, saw them, looked them over and then ignored them. She knew we were not hunting. Was it because it was spring or because we did not have a gun with us? Perhaps she read me, as the antelope and other prey read lions, and knew that I was not hunting. I know if it were fall and I was carrying the shotgun, sneaking up on these birds, she would have been at my side, quivering and giving a high pitched but soft whine. Dog and geese both seemed to know there was no danger here on this sunny, spring afternoon. Jake, the puppy, jumped up against me, and ran to Jill and chewed on her ear. He investigated new, interesting and mysterious things like deer droppings and sticks. He never saw the geese.

The big birds finally flew off when Jill began exploring out on the ice, and Jake finally noticed them as they left with a loud flapping of wings and loud honking. We continued our walk, and were no more than a hundred yards farther along when the pair of geese returned and landed just a stone's throw from where we had flushed them.

Over the next several days we had unseasonably warm weather. Temperatures soared into the seventies. It seemed as though the ponds went from totally iced-in to totally open water in record time. Strong south winds blew for several days and, no doubt, these winds were utilized by millions of birds on their journey northward. The small flocks and pairs appeared, and then in just a few days, I began to see the lone drakes. This is an indication that nesting is underway. The drake waits as his mate goes to the nest each day to lay a single egg. The pair stays together until the hen begins incubating or shortly afterwards, then she is on her own for the rest of the summer, unless she loses her nest and seeks out the male again. It seemed as if the normal, gradual buildup of birds, followed by the dispersal to nest sites, was abbreviated due to the sudden changes in the weather. First we had no birds, then a few birds, and finally just the local pairs. It all occurred in a very short time span.

On April 18, the blue-winged teal made their first appearance. This was just six days after I had seen the first mallard. There was a flock of seven—five drakes and two hens. The hens (blue-winged teal and other ducks) incubate the nest and raise the brood with no help from their mate. Incubation requires the hen to be on the nest almost constantly for nearly a month. She will only leave for brief periods, to feed, a couple of times each day. Always at risk, like all small birds and animals, there on the nest they are most vulnerable. They pay a heavy price. When you see flocks of ducks, you will see the great majority of the birds are drakes.

This little band of teal gave me a good show one morning. All seven were in Bear Country Pond, and I sat there in the early hours of the day with Jake and Jill. It appeared one of the hens in the little flock had chosen her mate, and these two remained just a little aloof from the others. The remaining hen seemed to be playing the dating game, as the other four drakes stayed close to her, bobbing their heads and making a little sound my keyboard cannot really describe. At one point, two of the hopeful suitors went beak to beak, each literally grasping the other's bill with its own, and sort of arm wrestling, but using bill and neck where hand and arm would be used with a human.

When I got up, they flushed, only to set down a stone's throw away in another pond. The teal are trusting birds. That is the polite way to say they are pretty stupid. They fly fast, though, and are a very sporting target. In the spring, when they are not being shot at, I have walked up on blue-winged and flushed them to another pool, walked up again and repeated the whole process until I had followed them around almost the entire property.

On April 19 and 20, things began to look more like normal. I began to see more small flocks of birds. The blue-winged band was still around, as was the ring-necked pair. Four pairs of green-winged teal began to hang around, as did small bands of wood ducks. Three pairs of the woodies and three pairs of hooded mergansers were about on the morning of the twentieth. Later in the day, I watched three hooded hens accompanied by a young drake that was not yet in full color. Most of the hooded merganser sightings were, as usual, on Big Pond.

In addition to the return of the migratory birds, a lot of the year-round residents reappear after a winter asleep in underground dens, down in the mud, or wherever it is they choose to snooze away the winter. The most notable of these, though not the most noticeable, is the black bear. The television news on April 17 featured footage of a bear that had wandered into a small town near here and holed up under a semi trailer.

Chipmunks, gophers and woodchucks poke their noses above ground in April and the odor of skunk may float to you on the breeze.

The most noticeable local critters in the spring are the tree frogs. Their spring courtship songs fill the air, and on some of the ponds, you can see the frogs floating motionless at the surface. A tiny frog head protruding from the water every twelve to eighteen inches. A defended territory perhaps? When the dogs or I get too close, the calling stops. If we continue to move closer, the heads drop out of sight all in unison, leaving the pond surface covered with circular rings as if a thousand raindrops hit the pond all at once, perfectly spaced.

The days passed, and spring slowly established itself. The air was filled with the sounds of the frogs, geese moving here and there, the winnowing of the snipe, and the morning and evening courtship flights of the woodcock. The booming of drumming grouse was a part of each sunrise, though there were fewer of the drummers this spring than there have been for several years. The haunting calls of the sandhill crane were heard nearly every day.

I spent some time "posting" for muskrats, armed with my shotgun. They had breached one of the dikes. Patch this as I might, I needed to bring justice to the enemy and prevent him from doing further mischief. One evening I sat quietly as the snow fell and began to cover the ground. A cold front was arriving. The pond I watched had held ducks nearly every time I had passed it for several days, but that evening there were none. I wondered if they knew somehow the pond would freeze during the night, and had moved elsewhere. It was very quiet. The sounds of the frogs were gone, save for two very hearty spring peepers that slowly called to each other through the evening. The snipe still flew and the woodcock began his ritual just at dark. I left without seeing any muskrat.

I was up late that night. At midnight, I went outside to check the weather. The deck was covered with snow, as was the ground. In the distance, out of the night, came the drumming of a grouse. Snow or no snow, cold or warm, day or night, this grouse was telling the world where he was. He was saying clearly that this particular log was his, and any lady grouse in need of affection could feel free to mosey on over.

Early the next morning, just after the sun had risen above the trees on the eastern horizon, I walked with the dogs around the circuit that included most of the ponds. The sunshine on the new snow was beautiful, and instead of looking up ahead of me as I walked, I looked down to watch for tracks. The yard was filled with rabbit tracks. The big snowshoe hare were now in their breeding season and there were several places where it looked as though two of the animals had been together or one had chased another. Certainly, it could have been that the two animals passed over that spot at different times, or even that the same rabbit had traveled the same route two different times during the night. However, if you have knowledge of the animal and its habits, you can read the sign and make reasonable assumptions. Everything I saw convinced me some mating or courting activity had gone on in the yard that night. The grouse that had drummed late into the night was still at it.

At Bear Country Pond, the water was open because of the depth of this particular pond and because there is good water flow through it. The little flock of blue-winged teal was here and it had grown to nine birds now. Ten wood ducks were also resting here, nine of them drakes. Only one pair of the green-winged teal swam the pond that morning, perhaps their brethren had continued on to the north. A pair of mallards jumped up from the flooded slough. During a second walk in late afternoon, the same area held thirty-five birds or more, mostly wood ducks. The snow from the night before was gone by afternoon. Winter wasn't giving up easily, but the battle was over now. Spring was here.

The Return is a wonderful time to be afield. We have written on our land a standing invitation to the waterfowl to stop in for a visit, or to stay for the summer and raise their family. The invitation is only visible from the air as the birds fly over. It is a tiny flyspeck on the map of the territory these birds cover in their semi-annual flights. It has taken us years to create this cluster of small, shining beacons lit by the sun's reflection off the water. What makes them pick this cluster? What determines if they will nest here or only visit? I neither know for sure nor do I care. I am just flattered each year that some of them accept.

April Storm

My routine, beginning in early April, was far different from any I had known. With my days free of commitments, I rose early and began with a walk, usually returning to the house in time to have a cup of coffee with my Alpha Female, just before she left for work. I would spend a little time trying to increase my contributions to the housekeeping duties. The three dogs seemed to enjoy having the boss home every day, and they got a lot more training time with him now that the he had no job. There were more things to keep busy with than I had ever imagined, but still I was able to keep very close watch on the activity on our property. It was the best part of a rather relaxing time.

We had had several snowy days and whenever there was snow covering the ground, I walked with eyes downward to see what tracks had been left overnight. One morning as the dogs and I walked the narrow trail that traversed the north side of the property, we came to a familiar stand of thick balsam. It is a favorite place for the deer to bed and for the birds to take shelter. The heavy layer of boughs breaks the wind and catches the snow. There, on the downwind edge of the conifer stand, were four snow-free spots on a landscape otherwise coated white. Four deer had bedded here while the snow fell. We had obviously moved them from their beds when we approached, and the dogs all got a nose full of deer scent as they investigated the scene. I had thought each of these snowy mornings would be the last of the year, but they just kept coming.

The last Saturday of the month arrived cold, windy, and yet again with snow in the air. Weather conditions do not often stop the outdoorsman from his chosen mission of the day, be it hunting, fishing or just patrolling some piece of ground. My duck-hunting parka and pants were made for days like this and are never buried too deeply in the closet. My morning walk took place on schedule, the dogs and I making a circuit of the property. The snow was melting as it hit the ground, so we could not observe tracks. At least I couldn't. The dogs did not need visual clues to know this animal or that had crossed the trail or tarried here or there. How wonderful it would be to have their sense of smell. To be able to test the breeze and know what was upwind, or to bend down, sniff the ground, and know what had passed by. We all have our silly fantasies.

We jumped ducks and grouse. Jill found the drummer that had been advertising himself almost constantly for the last three weeks and flushed him from his log. He sailed in front of me and landed in the same heavy balsam cover where we had found the deer beds a few days earlier. I tried to get Jake to notice him, but he thought I was trying to play. It was a nasty morning, but we sat for a few minutes in a couple of places just to see what we might see. However, back at the house there was much to do, so we returned and I dove into the project list. I was home alone for the weekend and it was a chance to catch up on some of these tasks. As I did, I looked frequently out the window. All day the snowfall had continued, getting heavier as the day went on. The snowflakes became larger and wetter. By early afternoon, the ground was covered and the snow depth was building. The wind was steady and strong. As I tackled the dishes and then pecked away at the keyboard, I could hear the wind howling over the house and through the pines in the yard. I wondered if ducks had gathered on some of the small, sheltered waters of my ponds. It was a day just like this several years ago, also in April, when I saw the biggest flock of wood ducks ever on the property. Nearly three dozen of these colorful birds had taken refuge on Big Pond to sit out that storm. There was work to do at the keyboard, but as the clock moved along, I knew I had to get outside once more before dusk. It was so hard to be inside when something interesting might be going on just beyond the limits of my vision.

Finally done, I got out the parka and called up the dogs. I shouldered my twelve-gauge pump gun as I had on the earlier walk. I had the gun set up with the super-full turkey choke, and I carried a half-dozen three-inch turkey loads. I had not yet seen a muskrat this spring, but had seen plenty of damage to the dikes from their tunneling. The turkey loads did a nice job on the rats. If I got a look at one of them, I would do my best to dispatch him.

I headed south from the house towards Big Pond and jumped some mallards there. I stood for five minutes watching the dark water, looking darker now because it was surrounded by snow-covered banks. I had often seen muskrat activity when there were weather conditions such as this, so I paused in hopes of catching one of them in the open. None of the little beasts showed. I continued south along the trail to its intersection with the road that runs straight east/west along the south end of the property. There, we turned west, towards the back field. Another pair of mallards flushed from the shallow, cattail-filled pond that lies alongside the roadway. The large wet snowflakes were now blowing into my face. When I reached the seven-acre opening of the back field, which has even larger fields and an open marsh near it, the breeze was much stronger. Now the wind-driven snowflakes made it hard to look ahead. A skunk's tracks crossed the road and I wondered what had brought him out of his den or shelter on a day like this. He was obviously no brighter than the dogs or myself. We crossed the field and entered the main trail, heading north. A hundred yards into the woods, the trail runs near the flooded slough and along the dike that keeps that area flooded. We moved along, trying to see ahead through the snow, the large wet flakes now almost blinding. We were nearly to Bear Country Pond, where the trail forks to pass on either side of it, when I paused for a moment. From here, I could see quite a lot of the pond as well as the new pond site. At least I would have been able to, but for the snow in my eyes. I spotted movement along the top of the new dike. There, I saw a long-tailed fox trotting along headed west. At first I thought it was a coyote because it was so large, but the overall shape said fox. This was the very same area where Rex had taken the shot at a fox on our varmint hunt earlier in the year. He had said it was a big one, so perhaps I was looking at the same animal.

It moved at a steady trot, glancing towards me now and again, but I couldn't say if it saw me or not. I suspect it did, for I was in the open and wearing brown wetland camo on a snowy white background with three dogs dancing around me. He looked much lighter than the average fox; almost tan like a coyote. It may have been an illusion created by the snow. He never slowed and disappeared behind one of the large brush piles left by the dozing operation. He apparently crossed the fence and entered the cedar swamp, for he did not reappear on the other side of the brush. As I walked on, a flock of a dozen or so ducks took wing from the slough, just across the dike from Bear Pond. They were not resting in their usual place, and that was explained by a story written in the snow. I saw the tracks of the fox, and it appeared he had come down to the edge of the pond where the birds normally feed and loaf. Perhaps he was hunting for them and had flushed them across the dike. Fox are efficient predators of ducks, especially of nesting hens. I thought perhaps I should try hunting this big fellow to save some ducklings and their moms. Maybe I would begin carrying my scope-sighted .22 instead of the shotgun on the off chance I would see him again.

I cleaned the snow off a lawn chair that had been set up behind a camouflaged screen earlier in the week, and took a break. The dogs snuffled as they pushed their noses into the fresh fox tracks, and Starr, the beagle, started up a rabbit. I sat for a half-hour as the sun went down and still it snowed hard. In the blind, I had my back to the wind and some alder brush behind me so it was not uncomfortable. Jake and Jill lay at my side; Jill constantly and Jake sporadically. Jake needed to get up occasionally to check the fox scent again or to attack a whippy raspberry stalk that had invaded his space. He was outside the blind doing just that when I heard the raspy quacking of a mallard drake coming towards me. Jake heard it too, and looked up as the big greenhead set his wings and dropped into the pond not twenty yards from me. He was even closer to the pup. He ruffled his feathers a bit after landing—as they always seem to do—and set to quacking. Jake looked at him with great curiosity and interest, tail up and wagging. He took several steps towards the duck, who paid no attention to him. When the dog got to the edge of the water, he sat down and stared at the bird as if trying to figure out what it was. Jake would move his head forward and lower it, then almost lean back. His ears would perk up and drop back down. Discovery is such a wonderful thing!

Finally, the pup lost interest. He trotted back into the blind just as a pair of wood ducks fluttered into the tree on the island. This was the tree where the wood duck box was attached. The drake left immediately, but the hen remained for several minutes seeming to look about her surroundings. I wondered if my old friend was back. This was the nest box where a particular woody hen had nested for four consecutive years. Eventually this bird flew off, and a few minutes later I saw two ducks come in low on the far end of the pond. It turned out they were wood ducks. A few minutes after they landed, the hen flew up and entered the nest box. Night was falling, along with the snow, so we packed up and walked back to the house. The noisy mallard took flight as we left. Starr had given up on the rabbit and rejoined us. Halfway home she found another. Again, she was using her voice to announce her find.

The following day the alarm was set for five, and when it started beeping, I switched it off and lay back down. It was already beginning to brighten outside, and I lay there debating with myself about sleep versus a nature walk. The dogs refused to help me decide, so I rolled out of bed. A bowl of cereal, a cup of coffee, then my three companions and I were again out of the house to make the rounds. We walked the exact trails that we had the previous evening but in reverse. Three inches of wet snow lay on the ground but no more was falling. The skies were gray and the wet snow clung to every branch of every tree. It was one of those mornings made for taking pictures if only the sun would emerge to brighten the landscape. The tracks of rabbits and a house cat traversed the back yard. My own tracks from the night before were nearly invisible, so it had snowed for some time after dark. The critter tracks had no snow in them at all.

On the main trail, a skunk had ambled along for several hundred yards; these tracks were fresh as well. I hoped not so fresh the dogs would catch up with him. The mixed flock of ducks was on the water where they normally rested and again we stopped in our blind for a short rest and observation period. When we moved along again, I spotted the tracks of a mink following the edge of the slough and later, fox tracks. Mr. Fox had been busy after our meeting, or perhaps it was another.

We did not tarry long on this walk. When we got back to the yard there were several robins bouncing around on the ground. They looked indignant over what Mother Nature had done to them yet again; dumping more snow on top of their banquet table and chasing their worms back underground. The ever-present geese were now calling and beginning to move around. They sleep late compared to the ducks and my dogs and me. The sun was coming out now, and it was already warm enough that the wet snow had begun falling from the trees. I dug for the camera in the hope of getting a nice Christmas card shot. No camera to be found.

By noon, most of the snow was gone. A few hours later, all signs of the April storm had disappeared.

May

The calendar does not neatly align itself with my own divisions of the year. The weather is variable from year to year, as we all know. But generally, my favorite weather of the year occurs in late April and early May, and then again in late September through early October. These are the times with plenty of cool mornings.

In May, new life is exploding forth. The earliest nesting songbirds, game birds and waterfowl are hatching their broods, provided that weather or predator has not claimed the nester, or the nest. If only the nest is lost, the bird will often try repeatedly to nest again. Ducks and grouse certainly are persistent in their effort to add more of their kind to the landscape.

On May 4, 2002, a family of whiskey jacks—also known as gray or Canada jays—flew into the mountain ash tree next to our house to raid food from the dog dish. The young were nearly as large as their parents, already flying like pros. Some of our summer birds had not arrived, but the jays had their brood out of the nest. On Mother's Day, the 12th, I spotted a hen pheasant alongside my driveway. She was probably lonely and unlikely to become a mother this spring, for it appeared no rooster had survived.

The light green of budding aspen and other plants begins to appear on the landscape in May. In hollow trees and underground burrows, small mammals give birth. My own activities outdoors take on a new urgency. The best days of spring are about to end. Soon, new foliage will make my wildlife viewing more difficult and clouds of mosquitoes will torment me. I resist using the smelly repellent. My pleasing walks in the woods become less frequent as the mosquito population explodes, eventually forcing me indoors. I go down fighting, but I do go down.

Duck Survey

My field notes and records show that the earliest date for an egg in one of my duck boxes was on April 7. The peak time period for "nest initiation" in the boxes is between April 14 and April 24. This ten-day period is when most nests welcome that first egg of the clutch. It is easy to come close on fixing the nest initiation date if you check the boxes regularly during the early part of the nesting season. The hen usually lays one egg per day. If you find X number of eggs on a particular day, deduct that many days from the date and you have the date the first egg was laid. Of course, this method does not work with a "dump nest." A dump nest is when more than one hen is dropping eggs in a single box. Dump nesting is very common among wood ducks and hooded mergansers as well as with other birds. All of the above could be learned by reading any of several books on waterfowl, but I think it is more fun to learn by actually doing it.

The first duck nest I found in one of my boxes was a big event for me. Box number one, on the island in Big Pond, was where it happened. This box had been set up for several years near Old Pond but had only been occupied by roosting flickers. I finally relocated it to the island in Big Pond and hung it about twelve feet up in a black ash tree. One day in 1992 I hauled a ladder out to the island, set it against the tree and climbed up. I tapped on the box as I always do. Countless times, I have nearly fallen off the ladder when, while checking a nest box, a flying squirrel or some other critter blasted out, nearly giving me a heart attack. Nothing happened when I knocked on the box, but when I unlatched and opened the door, frantic scratching came from inside. A hooded merganser hen blasted out of the entrance hole, croaking her dissatisfaction with me.

I was thrilled when I opened the door and found the clutch of eggs—creamy white and warm to the touch. Grayish-white down surrounded the eggs and ran up the sides of the box. The hen had pulled it from her breast to insulate her eggs. Had she left the box unhurriedly, she would have carefully covered the clutch with the down to hold in the stored heat. This clutch eventually hatched, and every year since, we have hosted nesting mergansers. Just as the books said, it sometimes takes a while to attract these birds to your artificial hollow tree. However, once you had them they were gonna be around every year, so long as you kept the boxes in place and maintained. The young birds that hatch in a manmade box also tend to nest in one when they are mature enough to breed. The females pick the nest site and tend to return to the area where they were hatched. I would imagine the mergansers nesting on Big Pond in 2002 are descendants of that first hen I met in 1992.

Before someone told me it wasn't legal, I often banded the hens I found in the nest boxes. A dozen hens were banded over the years. Half of these were never captured again. Four were recaptured once, one was recaptured twice and one woody hen was recaptured three times. The latter had nested four consecutive years in the same box, each year successfully hatching her brood. She is an old friend, at least in my eyes. I am quite sure she does not see me the same way, because she still hisses at me when I open the box and say hello each spring. The further along these birds are in the incubation period, the more reluctant they are to leave the nest. During the period when they are laying the eggs, they may only be in the box for a short period while they deposit the egg. If you happen to be checking the box at this time, they flush easily. As the clutch nears completion, the hen spends more and more time on it, and begins the process of pulling down from her breast to help insulate the eggs during the brief times she will

leave them to feed each day. As the hatch date nears, the hen is loath to leave her nest. Often, when I check a nest that is near hatching, the hen does not budge even when I reach down and gently pick her off the nest. It is as if she is clinging to the eggs in which she has so much invested. I check for a band and count the eggs. Even after placing the bird back on the nest and climbing down and leaving the area, the hen often remains on her nest.

I had raised wood ducks in captivity for years and it was an amazing thing to watch young wood ducks after they hatched. Even when hatched in an incubator, as my captive birds were, they have a programmed instinct to climb and jump. In the wild, the ducklings leave the nest after only a day or two. When the clutch is all dry and mobile, the hen will leave the nest and position herself immediately below it. There, she will call to her babes. The young ducklings coil themselves, look upwards to the entrance hole and launch themselves upwards, swinging one of their feet up to grab the vertical surface. Their tiny, sharp claws are designed for exactly this and their climbing ability is astonishing. It takes several jumps and the little one will sometimes hang there by one foot for a few seconds between leaps. It looks like they are resting, but it might be they are confused or perhaps taunting their siblings below who have not climbed as high. They are peeping constantly as if to cheer each other on, and the whole clutch can be up to the entrance hole in a very short time. They only pause for a few seconds, then launch themselves again, this time, out and away from the box. With tiny stubs of wings flapping, down they come to bounce off the ground below or splash into the water. They quickly lock in on mom and assemble near her.

My captive ducklings had no mom calling to them, but they still wanted to climb and jump. It seemed as though this jumping instinct stayed with them for many days, perhaps because they did not have an opportunity to go through the natural routine. Their brooder boxes had to be covered to prevent their escape. Even when feeding and watering them it required close attention, especially when opening the top of the brooder, to keep them from quickly scaling the side of the box and leaping out.

I once got the bright idea that if I let them go through this initial climbing routine, perhaps they would stop trying to escape the brooder. So I did one of those little stunts my Alpha Female finds so endearing, or is at least accustomed to. I ran about four inches of water into the bathtub. Then, I took a box and tied it up to the showerhead, six feet up the wall. (Actually, I first used one of Alpha Female's woven wood baskets, but she quickly took it from me.) I brought in a clutch of ducklings and put them all into the box. They promptly climbed up the sides and leaped out, splashing down in the bathtub. I cycled many ducklings through the jump school that year, but it didn't seem to dampen their instinct to escape from the brooder boxes. It did provide some entertainment for my family, however.

I have only seen wild ducklings leave a box on one occasion. While approaching a box to check it, the hooded merganser hen that nested inside had suddenly flushed out of the box. I pulled my canoe up close to the box, wedged the front end of it up on some hummocks, stood up and opened the hinged top. I was startled to see the entire clutch of eggs, save one, had hatched. I looked down into the faces of ten or twelve fluffy, hours-old mergansers. They were all staring right back at me. The one remaining egg was about to hatch. As I looked down at all those little upturned faces, I was alarmed to see some of the little balls of fluff were bent over, looking up and sort of wiggling their tails. This was exactly how the young captive raised wood ducks looked when they were about to start climbing. I was alarmed, for another programmed instinct in young ducks is for them to follow the first large, moving object they see after hatching. Nature intends this to be their mother of course. Sticking close to Mom gives them their best chance to survive those first hours out of the egg, so Mother Nature sees to it that the babies are programmed to do this. My dilemma for the moment was I feared these youngsters might leap out of their nest box and lock onto me.

I quickly closed the box and shoved the canoe out into the channel, trying to leave quietly. When I was twenty feet from the box, tiny mergansers began raining out of it, hitting the water with a little "splish." Fortunately, they stayed together in a tight cluster and did not seem to notice the canoe. I imagine they had already imprinted on their real mom, and the canoe neither looked nor sounded like her.

The little flotilla of downy mergansers soon swam down the channel and into some weedy cover. I hoped their mother would return soon and reunite with them, but I cannot be sure that happened. Later, I checked the box again and found the last hatchling barely alive. Just as I had often observed with my incubator-hatched birds, something was not right with this unfortunate little bird. Whatever was wrong had slowed its hatching and the energy he expended breaking free of the egg was more than he could handle. The birds that have trouble hatching are often just not strong enough to make it in the cruel, hard world. It is not unusual to find the body of one of these slow hatchlings when I am cleaning out the boxes after nesting season.

In late April, during one of my morning "stakeouts" at the ponds, I set up a little blind consisting of a lawn chair and some camouflaged fabric stretched between two alders. It was a cold morning, and much of the shallow water had iced over. I was watching Bear Country Pond because the little stream that flowed through it had kept most of the water open overnight. I had spread the contents of a pail of corn in the shallows a day earlier, as I often do in the spring, to attract ducks and geese. As the sun climbed above the horizon, I sipped a cup of coffee, poured from the little thermos I carried. I had the video camera along, but when I had turned it on it indicated the battery was near death. Likewise, with the extra battery I had brought along. I had not taken the binoculars that morning, so it was just going to be duck watching with the naked eye.

Some teal had been swimming around since I got there, never getting alarmed enough to leave while I set up the blind. More of their kind joined them in the semi darkness of the pre-dawn, and then a pair of wood ducks sliced into the still water and began preening and looking about the pond. Minutes later, another pair of woodies arrived. Instead of landing on the water, they fluttered into the branches of the large ash tree growing on the single island in the pond. They landed on one of the large branches right near duck box number two.

The hen had landed nearer to the box, perhaps two feet from it. She craned her neck and looked at the entrance hole. She would briefly glance here and there, and then turn again to look at the entrance to the box. I wished for my binoculars because I wanted to check for a leg band on her. There was no way I could pick it out at the distance we had between us in the dim light, but with binoculars, I might have done better. This is the box where my four-year wood duck hatched a brood each of the last four seasons. This might be her now. After a minute or two, the wood duck hen that was on the water fluttered up and landed on the limb only a foot from the hen already perched there. They stretched their necks out towards each other, shook their heads up and down and cussed at each other for five or ten seconds. Then, the bird that had been on the water fluttered towards her rival and drove her off the limb. They fluttered down into the water and the drake from the tree followed the gals down. The other drake swam over towards the row. The two couples made a lot of racket, shook their heads at each other and did some other posturing. So tacky, these neighborhood quarrels.

After a minute or two, things settled down and the two pairs began to swim about the pond, staying close—but not too close— to each other. Things were peaceful for a quarter-hour or more and other ducks came in to the pond to feed. I finished another cup of coffee then got up to head back to the house, flushing the mixed flock as I did. A day later, I again jumped a pair of woodies out of the tree as I walked by.

A day after that, I flushed three of them from the pond. That same evening, a lone drake patrolled the pond and I thought perhaps his mate was inside the box. I hoped so, and I hoped it would be my old friend. From the amount of wood duck activity around the box, I was sure there was a nest inside.

May 3 was the day of the year's first box survey. The front end of the canoe was tied to the back of the four-wheeler. A ladder was lashed to the canoe. My notebook rounded out the kit.

The first stop would be Bear Country Pond, to get a look inside box number two. I paddled the canoe out to the island and beached it there as Jill swam out to join me. The ladder was placed against the ash tree as quietly as possible. To reach the box, I have to climb to the top of the ladder, and then continue up another four or five feet using the limbs of the tree. When I got up to the box I stood on a thick limb and put my cap into the entrance hole to prevent any duck from escaping. I opened the top of the box, peeked inside and saw the form of a duck. She was sitting quietly on her clutch of eggs. I reached down and gently got my hand around her, thinking it must not be my old friend, for she had not greeted me with the customary hiss. When I lifted her, I saw shiny bands on each leg. I turned her to read the number on the right leg; 292. She had survived another round trip to the southern states and was back in box number two for the fifth consecutive year. I could not have been more pleased.

I did a tricky balancing act on the limb, holding 292 in one hand while I reached down into the box to move the ring of down so I could count the eggs. There were seventeen of them, and eight looked like merganser eggs. I put the bird gently back on her nest, closed the box and climbed down, remembering to remove my cap from the entrance. She never left the box after I sat her back on the eggs. It was nice to have her back.

I moved around the property checking fifteen of the boxes. The third box I checked had a single merganser egg buried in the wood chips that are in every box for nesting material. I suspected it had been abandoned because there were cobwebs across the entrance hole. After this, I found box after box with no sign of any activity in them, save for a few flicker feathers. The flickers often roost overnight in the wood duck boxes.

When I got to Big Pond, I was sure I would find merganser nests, but the first three boxes and the hollow tamarack had no sign of nesting. Even box number one, the box that had produced more young birds than any other, was empty. The last two boxes, numbers six and seven, are mounted high on ash trees and surrounded by water. I had seen a merganser leave number six, and always there seemed to be male mergansers on the water here. Number 6 had fourteen merganser eggs inside, warm to the touch and covered with down. Number 7 had eight merganser eggs, also covered with down but cool to the touch. Either the nest had been abandoned or the hen was still adding eggs to the clutch and not yet incubating.

I had hoped for better results than I found that day. The use of the boxes and their productivity had climbed for several years, peaking in 1998 when ninety-two eggs were laid in the boxes and eighty-seven hatched. In 1999, the egg total went up to 109, but many nests were abandoned or had eggs that did not hatch. Only seventy-seven young were produced that year, and since then the numbers have been much lower. I wish I knew why. Still, finding Ol' 292 again had made 2002 a year with at least some success in the nest boxes.

One Tough Duck

May 10, 2002, was a lovely spring day. The previous evening had been terribly windy with wet snowflakes in the air. We'd had cold and snow every few days for a long while and spring seemed reluctant to visit us, but the day dawned clear and cool with moderate winds. The ducks had been flying in and out of our ponds in good numbers for the past week. One morning, I spotted a hooded merganser hen perched atop box number one. As I watched her, a second hen flew out of the box. A few days earlier, I had checked this box and there was no sign of a nest, but now it appeared some late-nesting birds were continuing their hunt for the perfect home. Blue-winged teal were the most abundant birds on the property. It seemed their numbers had increased daily. Now, several of the ponds had pairs that seemed to have staked out nesting territory. A pair of ringnecks was seen, for several days running, in the open water around the big slough. I hoped they had found what they needed for nesting, for I had never raised a family of these little divers on the place before.

In the afternoon of that day, I walked to Bear Country Pond to spend a little time observing. My lawn chair and camo screen were still in place and I took a seat with my golden retrievers curled up on either side of me. A pair of blue-winged teal swam leisurely in the shallows and dipped their heads to feed. A cruising marsh hawk buzzed them, only six feet over their heads. The ducks and the raptor seemed to pay no attention to each other. I sat and watched through both the binoculars and the scope on the .22. I carried the gun on the off chance a muskrat or Mr. Fox would show themselves.

I had been sitting quietly for perhaps twenty minutes when I saw an animal swimming in the pond. My first thought was mink, but I shouldered the .22 quickly and tried to get the scope on it just in case it was a muskrat. Before I could pick it up in my scope, it dove and disappeared. I waited for several minutes and there it was again, swimming from shore to the little island in the center of the pond. It was a mink.

He hauled himself out on the island and began investigating every nook and cranny, as mink always seem to do. I lost sight of him as he worked his way along the shore. The blue-winged teal pair seemed to pay no attention to him and actually began swimming out towards the island where the little predator was prowling. Shortly, I saw the mink again as he came back along his own trail, but he reversed his field again and went out of sight. A flock of seven more teal pitched into the pond. I wondered if the mink might try to take one of these little ducks for its supper. That would be something to see.

A few minutes passed and I glanced up to the limbs of the ash tree that grows on the island. A pair of birds began hovering around the tree. The sun was behind the birds so I was not able to identify them. It seemed as though they were hovering around the wood duck box in the tree, the one where wood duck hen 292 was incubating her clutch of seventeen eggs.

The birds seemed agitated, and I soon saw why. The mink had climbed the tree and was on a limb near the front of the duck box! As happens once in a great while, it looked as though I might witness one of nature's little dramas.

Normally, in a situation like this, I try to be only an observer. If you do not interfere, you will see things as they happen in nature, and when that happens, I consider myself lucky indeed. However, what I was watching that evening was a drama that involved a duck with which I had a long history. Hen 292 had nested in this box the four previous years, and she was well along in her incubation of the fifth clutch of eggs she had produced here. She might be on the eggs right now, in fact most likely she was, because she would only leave the box perhaps twice each day for brief feeding periods. I had a scope-sighted .22 in hand, and the range was about thirty yards. It would be a fairly easy shot to take out the mink. Nevertheless, mink are a part of the landscape here, and I enjoy the predators almost as much as I enjoy the ducks. They are my allies in the muskrat wars. I was on the horns of a dilemma.

The two songbirds soon left the scene, and the mink entered the duck box. I listened for sounds of a struggle inside the box but heard none. My ears being what they are, that didn't mean there wasn't a death struggle going on. No wood duck hen came out of the box. What should I do?

I decided to get involved. I don't know if it was the right choice or not, but I made my decision. I rested my elbows on my knees and let the scope settle on the upper corner of the duck box, the corner away from the entrance hole. I would try to drive the raider away.

At the crack of the little rifle, the teal exploded into flight. The sleepy retrievers jumped up and looked around. I had heard the smack of the slug hitting the duck box, but there was no sign of any reaction—neither from the mink that was in the box, nor the duck that might be. After ten seconds or so, the mink emerged and crawled out onto a limb near the box, looking around and appearing a little confused. I put another shot into the limb he was perched on, and he began scrambling down the trunk. When he was five feet off the ground, he hesitated. I put another shot into the tree trunk right behind his tail, and he leaped off the tree to the ground.

I sent Jill out to the island. I wanted to put a real fright into this critter in hopes he would not return. She swam out to the island and began snuffling around. I gave her the dead bird command and she worked back and forth over the little island, her nose obviously full of the scent of a real funny smelling bird.

A few years before, a young beaver had taken up residence in this pond. It had started to build a lodge on the island. He had an underwater entrance and had piled up mud and sticks over this for a week or so before he decided there must be greener pastures somewhere else and left the pond. It appeared the mink had taken refuge in this old beaver lodge. Jill began dismantling it. She dug furiously in several different spots and it looked as though she had the mink scent for a while, but eventually began looking perplexed. I called her off and hoped we had frightened the little predator away for good. Knowing what I do of these animals, I thought it unlikely he would stay away now that he had been inside the box and knew its potential for a meal.

I walked back to the house and wondered about 292. Had she been inside and fended off the mink or had she been away feeding? She may well have been killed in defense of her nest while I sat thirty yards away. A loss of the clutch of eggs, or part of it, was probably the best I could hope for, and I would have gladly settled for that if I knew this long-lived and productive hen had survived. I would have to wait until morning to find out.

My attention had been drawn to the marauding mink by the two songbirds that hovered around the duck box that evening. Many birds make it a habit to raise an alarm when a predator is present. A common occurrence I see is when crows mob an owl. When these noisy birds see an owl, they sound an alarm and every crow within hearing seems to rally to the mob. It is hard not to notice when one of these assaults is in progress, for the crows raise an unbelievable ruckus and it's clear they are mad. If you hear such a thing, watch the sky and you will see crows converging from all directions, at full speed, on the noise. I've watched the poor owls flying low and weaving through the trees, trying to lose the small cloud of crows that is flying above him. Blue jays and even chickadees will raise a fuss when they see a predator as well, warning any other critter that will listen, that there is danger about. That evening, this behavior had worked to call my attention to the duck box. I wondered if it had done any good for 292.

I was up early the next day and out of the house before 6:00

A.M. I would need both my ladder and the canoe in order to check box two and the fate of my favorite wild duck. Both were at the other end of my nest box trail. I thought I might as well check the boxes at that end as long as the gear was there, and then work my way over to box two. I drove the ATV to box number seven, which is in the flooded swamp near Big Pond. I had the ladder there and I had found a hooded merganser nest of eight eggs just eight days earlier.

I waded into the flooded grass, carrying the ladder and set it up against the ash tree that held the box. When I got near the box, I stuffed my hat into the entrance hole as I always do, and carefully opened the hinged top. Inside I saw a pile of feathers. I reached down and fished them out. It was the remains of a hooded merganser hen. There was no carcass, but the end of one wing was there with a few of the primary feathers still attached. I looked down from the ladder to see if I could spot a carcass but there was no sign of it. Jill was sloshing around and probably would have brought it to me if she came across it. There were nine cold eggs in the nest, so the bird had added one egg since May 3, and had then perished, dooming her clutch of eggs as well. I tossed the eggs into the water and cleaned the box. I was concerned as I moved to box six, just fifty yards away.

I had never lost a nesting hen inside one of the boxes before; at least I had never seen evidence of it. Now I had watched a mink invade a box, and a quarter-mile away, I had found another box attacked by a predator. Few of my boxes had any sort of predator guard, which many people attach to the tree or post to keep terrestrial predators from climbing to the box. I had been lucky for many years but had always worried a crafty mink, marten or raccoon would find a meal in a box someday and then begin systematically hunting the whole string of boxes. It looked like my nightmare might now be real.

As I climbed up to box seven, I was relieved when a hooded hen flushed out of it. She and her clutch of fourteen eggs were safe. I continued on my way checking several other boxes. I finally got to Bear Pond and paddled out to the tiny island where box two hung on the lone black ash tree that grew there. I looked over the old beaver lodge that Jill had torn apart when she hunted for the mink, and saw the bullet hole in the tree from my third shot. I climbed up, stepped from the ladder onto the limbs of the tree and saw another bullet scar where I had shot into the limb where the mink had been perched. I put my stocking cap into the entrance hole, took a breath and opened the box.

She had died on her precious clutch of eggs. Her body was in the incubating position, and the mink had attacked her head, probably killing her quickly with a bite to the neck. The head was completely gone, and the hungry killer had chewed his way down into the body cavity starting at the neck. One egg had been pulled from beneath her body and the end of it broken off. By the amount of feeding that had occurred on the carcass, either the mink had returned during the night to feed or he had killed her some time before I had seen him the previous evening, and when I did see him he was returning to feed. I suspect the latter for the eggs were all cold. If the hen had died during the time I had watched the mink, the eggs probably would have retained some heat because of the warm down that surrounded the nest and the insulating body of the bird. I carried her down to the ground with me.

The nest had been a dump nest, more than one bird having laid eggs there. For that reason, I did not clean out the box on the off chance the second hen might return to incubate it. This was not likely, but a possibility. On the ground, I examined 292 and saw where her breast looked sort of like a bad haircut from her pulling out down to insulate her eggs. She seemed to have been in good condition with good weight on her body. I removed the bands, one on each leg, and I buried her inside that old beaver lodge where Jill had dug the side open. As I paddled back to shore, I said aloud, "Good try little bird."

Wood duck hen 292 had incubated fifty-seven eggs in the same box over five springs. She had reached, or was about to reach, what was at least her fifth birthday. Five times she had made the successful round trip from Minnesota to her wintering grounds (likely somewhere between Missouri and the gulf coast), surviving the guns of autumn and daily exposure to predators and the weather. She had hatched at least thirty-two young birds, some of them hers and some of them hooded mergansers. I have lost some of my notes from 2001 when she was on a nest of fifteen eggs, but as I recall most of these hatched as well, so her duckling count was probably well over forty. She may have nested elsewhere before finding her favorite spot on the island in Bear Country Pond. By any measure, she had done her share in the perpetuation of her kind. She had also provided me with a lot of entertainment for five springs.

The mink that killed my favorite wild duck is simply a predator doing what nature intends. He may be my ally in my muskrat war, for my ponds seem to be almost empty of muskrats this spring, perhaps partially because of this same mink. This will save some of my wild rice, which will feed some more ducks, and more ducks will likely feed me, the mink and other predators. The loss of 292 is something I feel a bit of sadness over, but that is just human nature. Each day, such incidents are happening a thousand times over, all around us in the natural world. Many of 292's offspring are probably on nests right now within a few miles of here. However, for me, something will be missing next spring. There will be no opportunity to meet again with my wood duck hen number 292.

Duck hunters have a tradition of saving any duck bands they collect from birds they have killed and displaying them on the lanyards of their duck calls. Some of the men I hunt with in Arkansas have the entire lanyard sheathed in aluminum bands. My own lanyard looks silly compared to those. I have two duck bands and one goose band. One of the duck bands was taken from a pen-raised bird I released one spring and then shot (not knowing it was one of mine) the following autumn. These "pro" duck hunters with all the bands would scoff at anyone decorating their lanyard with bands from birds they did not themselves shoot, so I haven't added any phony trophies. However, on the day I found 292 dead on her nest, I affixed her band on my lanyard. If anyone asks me about the legitimacy of my band collection, I will own up I did not kill the duck that wore that one particular band. When I am able to tell them the bird's life story, my guess is they will agree it is fitting and proper for her band to be displayed among my trophies.

June and July

In June, the hordes of mosquitoes are upon us. The frosty mornings that kept their numbers down in early May are gone until September. Spring rains have normally saturated the ground and made every depression into a pool that will grow mosquitoes.

The forest is covered in green, which pleases my wife, who delights in the light green color of the new buds and leaves. I enjoy the appearance of the landscape but miss the better visibility I have when the trees are bare. I like to see things. Many of the birds are hatching their young in June, and the activity around the nest increases as the adult birds are on the move constantly supplying food for their brood.

As I walk the edges of the ponds now, if I am stealthy enough, I will see the first broods of ducklings. When I walk along the trails to and from the ponds, I may encounter a brood of grouse and perhaps witness the hen grouse performing her broken wing act in hopes of leading me away from her family.

In July, the weather usually is the driest of the year, with temperatures rising to where I find it uncomfortable at times. The windows are open at night and the sounds from outside tell us the time of year. The sounds of crickets and the buzzing of insects have replaced the sound of the spring frogs. My walks in the woods become fewer and shorter due to heat, lack of visibility, and bugs.

Though walks for pleasure are now at a minimum, the dry weather of July combined with the thirst of growing trees and plants will dry the soil and lower the groundwater level. One can drive a pickup now in places usually not accessible. It is usually a good time of year for excavating work because of the dry soil. There is always such work to be done.

Gosling Reprieve

The message on the answering machine said it was an opportunity to broaden my horizons. Bob Davis, a friend from the local chapter of the Minnesota Waterfowl Association, was hauling another load of goslings to a new home. He wondered if I would be interested in lending a hand. I thought it a fine idea.

As mentioned in a previous chapter, our local MWA group has been very involved in the goose relocation program. That program has resulted in an abundance of nesting geese throughout the state. There are so many geese that there are few places left in the state where goslings are welcome. The program may become a victim of its own success.

Bob Davis has been one of the shakers and movers who made the relocation effort work. He has been directly involved with moving over 12,000 geese since the early 1990s. Besides moving birds to various parts of Minnesota, thousands have been released in Louisiana, Missouri, Iowa and the Dakotas.

During that time, I had obtained geese for release on my own property. At three different times I released groups of five or six birds at various locations on my place. The first group disappeared immediately. The day I released them was the last time I saw them. Neighbors reported a band of young geese walking along the shoulder of the nearby state highway. Perhaps my geese hitchhiked back to Minneapolis. The next time I released birds, they too, promptly left the site that I thought best for them. These however, traveled cross-country, through the woods, and ended up on Big Pond. They spent the summer there, even returning occasionally after they learned to fly.

My third group of birds was released on Big Pond. It had been good enough for geese the previous year, for they had sought out this pond and then stayed put. This third group promptly moved to the pond that the first two groups had immediately abandoned. I guess geese just do not like being told what to do.

Some of the birds were wearing numbered neck collars that could be read if you got close enough. Later in the summer, I checked the numbers on the collars and found only one bird was from the group I had released! I checked in with my neighbor, Bernie, who had also released birds. His flock had disappeared he said, but he had the numbers from the collars. Sure enough, some of his birds had hoofed it over to my place, a mile away. I didn't

have all of Bernie's geese, but at least three of them were here. We had released eleven birds at the two sites. Now, there were five birds on my pond. There were three from Bernie's group, and one from mine. Another, without a neck collar, may have been from either. What happened to the others is a mystery, and why the groups reformed is another. I wondered if perhaps the two groups of released birds each contained birds from a single family. Geese have strong family bonds, and obviously, they are able to communicate in a way that allows them to recognize their family. It is also obvious they hear very well. Could it be that a separated family was able to hear each other from a mile away and regroup? It would be interesting to know.

For the time being, I will not be able to release any more city geese on my property. The Minneapolis geese that are rounded up in the future will mostly be slaughtered. Some are processed and donated to local food shelves, but at a cost of $8.00 per bird for processing, it is an expensive proposition. The rest will likely be killed and deposited in landfills. An obvious solution to minimizing such waste would be to liberalize our already liberal goose hunting seasons. There are some concerns with the idea, for while increased harvest of the local populations is needed, it must be done in such a way that it will not increase the harvest of migrant populations of geese. Those populations are not at a level that will allow increased harvest. We now have special early seasons that are designed to protect the migrant populations. These seasons would need to be started earlier, run later, and include less restriction. It is a thorny issue, especially with the bunny huggers fighting intelligent management every step of the way.

So, my own work with geese and my association with the local MWA chapter prompted the call from Bob. There were currently hundreds of geese sitting in pens at the Carlos Avery Wildlife Management Area just north of Minneapolis. Some were to be transported to Indian Reservation land in Minnesota, and some to Iowa. I was unable to help with the first run, but eagerly accepted Bob's invitation to haul a load of birds to Iowa.

I met Bob at his home at 5:30 A.M., and from there we drove his pickup to Carlos Avery. There, we had help from DNR personnel and other volunteers. I definitely got the impression that nearly all of these folks had seen and handled too many geese. Nobody seemed to be enjoying themselves as much as I was. In spite of this, we had little trouble in loading 294 geese, seven to a cage, onto our specially designed trailer. A few adults were bound for a special study. The rest were "fuzzies" (young birds still covered with down) or juveniles that already had feathers. A second vehicle and trailer, with DNR personnel, had an equal number of birds and was bound for the same destination in Iowa. We were on the road by 8:30 A.M. in our two-vehicle caravan.

We were to link up with Iowa DNR people at a wayside rest, just across the Iowa border. These folks would then lead us to the release site. I was under the impression that from the rendezvous point, we would travel another twenty miles south along the freeway, then approximately eight miles east. On our drive to the border, Bob filled me in on the history of Geese Unlimited and his own experiences with the group. It was a pleasant drive and a beautiful summer day.

At the wayside, one fellow from the Iowa DNR took ten or so of the adult geese that were bound for the study. A second man was to lead us to the primary release site. We followed his truck south. The mileage estimates I had been given were just a tad shy of the real story. We drove about fifty miles south before we exited the freeway. My hopes that the "eight miles east" estimate was correct were dashed when we seemed to keep driving and driving. We drove for perhaps another forty miles. Bob and I began to wonder if our guide was just cruising the countryside looking for a suitable release location. We finally turned south again, then east on a gravel road. Now, we must be getting close, we thought. We drove for another ten minutes or so, and the road became two ruts. I saw signs marking the boundary of the Big Marsh Wildlife Management area.

The two ruts became a grass-covered dike. We drove along this for over a mile. I kept looking for some sort of facility. I thought we were to be joined by people who would band the geese and move them to holding pens. As it turned out, we stopped on a spillway in the middle of the dike, and there we were to unload the geese. It would be just the five of us, and no banding was to be done.

It took us approximately ninety minutes to unload our charges, with one man grabbing geese from the cages and handing them, two at a time, to the other four of us. We walked the birds to the shoreline and let them go. Perhaps one in five of them turned away from the water and bolted back up the side of the dike. Stubborn birds.

It was warm, and it was tiring. We were able to accomplish the mission suffering only minor scratches. Bob got it the worst and lost a bit of blood. He had told me to be sure to wear a long sleeved shirt for exactly this reason. He had on a short-sleeved shirt. Evidently, he wanted to demonstrate that he knew what he was talking about.

We headed north, and I got home about 9:30 P.M. I was tired and sunburned. I had driven and ridden 750 miles and had been up since 4:00 A.M. But I felt good. I had learned something, collected a new experience and helped to give over 500 geese a sporting chance. My horizons had, indeed, been broadened.

Jake and Jill II

The puppy named Jake was seventeen weeks old when May rolled around and I took him in for his checkup with the vet. He weighed forty-two pounds, and I was told he would likely double that weight by the time he quit growing. His feet seemed to grow before your eyes and he was as tall as Jill, (who weighs sixty pounds at the most) by early May. By the end of August, his weight was up to eighty-five pounds.

His training had gone well, though there will be training to do for a long while yet. "Sit" and "stay" were mastered early and the "come" command he knew quite well, though he began to obey it only when it suited him. That was cured with a twenty-five foot rope attached to his collar. We were on a walk and I had the rope coiled up at first, using it as a short leash to reinforce the "heel" command. We stopped and played a bit and I tossed training dummies for him for several minutes, and then let him play on his own while I sat and watched. The rope was still on his collar with the other end in my hand. When he was occupied with wrestling a whippy stick, I told him to come. Of course, he acted as if I had said nothing and continued with his game. I called his name to be sure he knew I was talking to him. When he looked at me I repeated the come command. He turned back to chew the stick and I said, "COME!" and reeled him in with the rope. He didn't like that very much but I praised him when he got to my side. I repeated this one more time. After that, when I called him, he would turn and run to me.

Much like Jill, Jake did not seem very keen on chasing a training dummy when he was very young. A ball or a chew toy got his attention but not the dummy. Like Jill, in time, he learned to love chasing the dummy and he got plenty of opportunity to do so. It was amazing to watch him learn, and almost as amazing to me that I could teach him.

His first swim was pretty entertaining for me, and a little frightening for him. We were on a walk and I had been tossing a dummy for him. When we got to one of the ponds, I began to toss it into shallow water and he seemed happy to splash in after it. I tossed the dummy into a little deeper water each time and Jake would wade after it, seeming just a little concerned, as the water got deeper. Finally, I tossed it to a point just past where he could wade after it. He waded out and stretched his neck but the waves he created, along with the breeze, pushed the dummy slowly away from him. The next thing you know he was swimming and it seemed like he had been swimming his whole life. He caught up to the dummy about fifteen feet from shore and grabbed it in his mouth with no hesitation. When he turned around, saw me up on shore and saw all of that water between the two of us, his eyes got big. Then it looked as though he was trying to climb up on top of the water. His front paws began coming far out of the water, splashing loudly with each stroke. His forward progress was slowed by the inefficient strokes and that seemed to panic him a little, his paddling getting even more desperate. I wished for my video camera.

For a while after this, every time he swam it was with the noisy, slow, flailing paws, even though his very first swimming strokes had been those of a pro. It took him just a little while to start keeping those paws under water.

Jake continued to be a very mild-mannered and well-behaved dog. He loved being around us, but for the most part, did not torment us seeking constant attention. The Alpha Female loved to hold him in her lap, but it was not long before she couldn't easily pick him up and put him there. His color remained blonde, the color of Arkansas rice stubble. He loved the other two dogs, and he tormented our docile Jill for several hours each day. Jill was very patient.

There would be some setbacks in Jake's training. Dogs go through times when they seem to lose their heads, just as adolescent humans do. Only after he has a hunting season behind him will I dare to make a guess as to what kind of hunter he will be. However, even if he were to fail miserably in the field, he will own us for the rest of his life.

Jill displayed the patience of a saint with the new puppy. She is a very easygoing dog. Even when doing retrieves on dummies, with Jake trying to get between the two of us to pull the dummy from her mouth, she never growled or got cross with him. At first, she could just force her way to me, pushing him aside. However, as he grew, she had to outmaneuver him. In their "leisure" hours, the two dogs were together most of the time, though Jake often preferred to be with the people of the house instead of the dogs. Jill would sit on the front steps for hours, but Jake needed to say hello to my wife or myself every hour or so. At her worst, Jill just ignored the pup. At her best, she played with him as though she was a puppy herself, though she let him be the energetic one. She would lie on the floor and let Jake climb all over her as they playfully chewed on each other, showing that fake snarl as they sparred. It was not unlike watching my son and grandson wrestle on the floor.

When I trained Jill, she and I had a distinct advantage over what Jake and I have now. I was raising game birds at the time Jill was a puppy. I had several kinds of North American ducks as well as pheasant and chukar. Whenever I lost a bird to disease or accident, I froze it and we then used these during the dog training. There was also plenty of opportunity to work with live birds. I released pheasant throughout the year; both to train the dog and to just have them around. Besides my own fields, my neighbor, Mike, owns a Christmas tree farm. It has cover ideal for the birds, with areas of wild hay, closely packed conifers, and weed-choked roadways between the trees. These weeds are loaded with seed the pheasant relish. Mike has always been kind enough to let me hunt his ground or to work the dog there.

Pheasant seem to be Jill's favorite bird to hunt. She is wild about the big birds, and she gets plenty of opportunity to hunt them most years. A few days after release, the birds seem to act nearly as wild as those hatched in nature do. It is great training for the dog to hunt them, and they are fine to eat as well. My favorite time to hunt them is in the late fall when there is just a bit of snow on the ground. Jill makes quite a picture, quartering back and forth to test the breeze, her golden coat contrasting with the white landscape. Add a rooster pheasant to the picture, rising in front of the dog with its long tail waving behind it and cackling like that tail is on fire, and you know why men hunt pheasant.

My six seasons of hunting with Jill have given me great satisfaction. Watching her work is now one of the most enjoyable ingredients of my hunting experience. She has her faults, to be sure. She dawdles too much when returning a bird, especially if the bird is alive and if she can see me. She puts live birds down to rearrange them in her mouth and has lost a couple of ducks that way when they took the opportunity to dive under water. However, she is well mannered in the blind or in the living room, and everyone who meets her seems to be impressed with her sweet nature. As a hunting dog, I know she finds birds that many dogs would not.

Late in the duck season in 2000, Jill and I made a hunt on the Bowstring River north of the town of Deer River. It was a foggy morning and unseasonably warm. We launched the canoe in the darkness and paddled downstream a couple of miles to an area a short distance upstream from where the river empties into Bowstring Lake. Here was a wide, shallow marsh filled with wild rice. In a large, circular opening just off the main river channel, we set up a couple dozen decoys and hid in some brush just at first light. A few ducks were flying but none seemed interested in our decoys. The fog was so thick that the birds flying within range were there and gone so quickly that I never got off a shot. We sat for two hours, and then I decided to pick up and paddle around.

I paddled out and began picking up the blocks. As usual, when you have lowered your guard to do something, ducks came by. A pair of ringnecks passed at thirty-five yards and I managed to get up my gun and knock down the drake. He came down at a forty-five degree angle and I tracked him with the gun as he did, planning to shoot him again as soon as he hit the water. He was obviously alive and I wanted to get another shot into him before he could dive and escape. These ringnecks are awfully tough birds.

When he hit the water, he skipped off it like a flat stone! He bounced up onto shore, so I sent Jill and began paddling over.

When I got to shore, Jill was already all over the duck scent, but I was surprised she did not have the bird. On dry land, she never misses a bird. I got out of the canoe to help and discovered the problem. The bank was undermined with a maze of muskrat tunnels, and there were holes leading down to these tunnels. Some had been dug by muskrats or perhaps by animals going after muskrats, and there were places where duck hunters had stepped, their weight collapsing the thin layer of covering soil into the tunnel. Our duck had found its way into one of these.

I encouraged Jill with the "dead bird" command as she snuffled and searched here and there for scent. I coaxed her with encouraging words, but thought the duck was lost. At times, she got "birdy" as if she was on scent, but then seemed to lose it. We kept this up for about ten minutes, and then I sat down and watched for other ducks while letting Jill continue her search. After another ten minutes or so, I called her over and had her sit at my side. I considered the cripple to be a lost cause.

I managed to knock down a couple more ringnecks. One drake came down far out in the pool, and even after several long shots at him he was able to reach the far shore. Why he chose shore as his hiding place, rather than to dive, I do not know. It was his last mistake. I sent Jill across and directed her to where I had seen the bird reach the shoreline. She crawled out on the bank and had the scent immediately. I saw her pause and then pounce, coming down with her front feet together just as you may have seen fox and coyotes do when they hunt mice. Her head went down, up it came with the drake and she made the long return trip to me with the bird.

We sat for perhaps another ten minutes until I decided to get back to picking up the rest of the decoys and move on. I thought it wouldn't hurt to let Jill look for that lost cripple for a little while longer while I picked up the blocks. I sent her, with a hand signal, to the last area she had seemed to have the scent of the bird. I gave her the "Dead bird! Fetch 'im up!" command, and she began hunting for scent. Out of curiosity, I watched and was surprised to see her get birdy right away. Instead of picking up the decoys, I paused to enjoy one of my favorite things in hunting, watching my dog work. She would seem to have scent and then lose it. She would stop to listen and then sort of half pounce to a new area. Finally, I realized she could both hear and smell the bird as it swam around in the muskrat tunnels. It seemed like it was only sporadically that she detected the cripple, but nonetheless, she was still in pursuit. She worked farther and farther away from me, and was fifty yards from where the duck had landed. She had been working for at least ten minutes. Then I saw her pounce and begin to dig. She dug furiously for ten seconds, and then her head went down. I did not dare to hope. Up came that beautiful golden head with a ring-necked drake dangling from her jaws. She held him by the head, which she seems to want to do with crippled ducks, and she pranced back to me, the duck swinging back and forth with her gait. How she managed to track that bird in water-filled tunnels is beyond me, much less how she pinned it in a place where she could dig for it. I imagine the bird eventually wedged itself into a tight spot and was too weak to extricate itself.

I hollered praise all the way as my dog trotted back. Her head was held high. A lot higher than it needed to be, if done only to keep the duck from dragging. She was proud of what she had done, and if she was proud, then I was fit to bust.

At first, I thought perhaps this was another crippled duck. I am quite sure now it was the one I knocked down. Anyone who loves their dog can imagine the praise I now showered on Jill as I took the duck from her. She sat there panting and "smiling," letting me scratch her. She knew she had done something praiseworthy, and praise she got.

I could tell you some amazing tales of Jill's retrieves, for there are many. However, I will spare you from further shameless bragging.

These days when I walk to the mailbox, I have two escorts. Jill walks at heel on my left, Jake on the right. I am the book and they are the bookends. If I say, "sit," they sit, and wait patiently side by side as I walk on, staying until I call them. In the evening, the two of them, along with our ornamental beagle, Starr, are usually curled up near me wherever I happen to be.

It is too early to tell whether Jake will one day pull crippled ducks from underground tunnels. However, watching him learn the trade, with Jill there to help, is going to be a whole lot of fun.

August

The first signs of autumn, in my part of the world, appear in mid-August. At least the first signs that I notice. Two of those signs in particular are hard for anyone to miss. The migration of the nighthawks begins in August, and these seldom-seen birds suddenly appear in numbers during daylight hours. Their flight is somewhat like that of a bat and even more like a swallow. Like the bat and the swallow, they feed on insects while the birds themselves are in flight. Up close, they are handsome birds with distinctive white bars across their wings, but they appear drab at a distance. Some years, their flight lasts for a week or more. Other years, they grace the skies for only a day or two. When the latter, they are usually in great numbers. I suppose they must migrate while there are still plenty of flying insects along the route, for fuel. It seems logical that the more concentrated flights occur when a sudden cold snap to the north wipes out the flying insects on which the birds depend. I will need to look that up one day.

The second sign that is hard for me to miss is the changing of the balsam poplar leaves. This lowland cousin of the aspen starts to change its color early, the leaves becoming dull brown. There is a lot of balsam poplar near my home, so I see this subtle change immediately.

Usually, the beginning days of August, and perhaps much of

the month, are dry compared to every other month, save July. We often get a break from the mosquitoes in August, but those that do show themselves during this month are the small and very aggressive variety. I have heard that we have many varieties of these little pests, but to me there are August mosquitoes and there are all the rest.

The tree swallows that filled the skies in June, have, for the most part, left the area. Families of bluebirds are still about and will soon begin forming into larger flocks for their journey south. Fireweed is probably the most noticeable blooming plant to show itself during this slice of the calendar. The mast crop, such as there is in this part of the world, is ripening, but the red squirrels will already be testing the acorns on the burr oak. It seems these little critters don't mind their acorns "rare."

The retrievers and upland dogs will likely get some work that is more intense than any they have seen through the rest of the off-season. Their masters are thinking about grouse season and trying to make up for lost time. A few trips to the sporting clays range is on all of our "to do" lists. However, if you are like me, you will work the dog more than you will shoot. The dog will be a lot sharper than you are, come opening day.

Fishing is the Pits

Despite the title of this book, it is obvious by now that it describes much more than hunting and hunting-related subjects. Perhaps it would be more fitting to call it **An Outdoorsman's Year**. I chose to use the word hunter over outdoorsman because I consider myself, first and foremost, a hunter. My other interests in nature were triggered, more than anything else, because of my experience as a hunter. All hunters are outdoorsmen, but not all outdoorsmen are hunters, and I am happy to be both.

I do not consider myself a fisherman. As a lad, I did my fair share of fishing and I enjoyed it, and found particular pleasure in fishing for stream trout. Fishing lakes for trout was almost as good. Eventually my widening interests in other outdoor pursuits conspired with the demands of my life as a husband, father and breadwinner. Fishing was pushed so far down the list of things I liked to do that I pretty much gave it up. That being said, this book would not be complete without at least one fishing yarn.

When my sons were ten and twelve, I got back into fishing for a few years in order to spend time with them on what I consider a healthy and worthwhile pursuit. As they grew older, they began to spend more time on other interests and when they did fish, they generally did so with their pals. I made the odd fishing excursion every now and again, but it has been several years since I even purchased a license. Even with such a limited amount of time invested in fishing, I have had some memorable trips over the years. During several trips to Michigan, I fished with my cousin, Chas, on the Yellow Dog River. "The Dog" was one of the favorite fishing spots for both his dad and mine. We fished in a wilderness area, far from the sound of chain saws or lawn mowers, and the trout we caught were beautiful, native brook trout.

Some of the best fishing I have had in Minnesota took place in the month of August, when for two or three years I did some trout fishing within an hour of my home.

My home lies just south of Minnesota's Mesabi iron range. The Mesabi Range has been exploited for its treasure for most of a century now. The iron mining brought about the settlement of the area and has been the economic engine for the people of the range and, to a degree, of the entire state. The land bears the scars. Mountains of "tailings" lie close against some of the small towns and the dormant mine pits are ugly gashes in the landscape.

Today our laws require the people who mine the land come back to repair it. While it's hard for me to know if the repaired land will be as fruitful as it might have been if left untouched, I realize that people need resources from the earth. I'm glad the repair work is required. Those tailings piles and man-made canyons are here because in the past, the mining operations were allowed to cut and run, once the profit potential was gone. So we are left with those monuments to exploitation and the people here have grown accustomed to them. Occasionally, efforts are made to repair or hide some of these scars, or at least make the best of the situation. One such effort was to plant game fish in some of the old pits that were now filled with water. Not a bad idea. Not quite the same as catching native game fish in the Boundary Waters Wilderness, but a pit with trout in it beats a pit without them.

A couple of my coworkers liked to fish in general, and fish for trout, in particular. They were fishing one of the old mine pits hard, and I followed their reports closely. The trout in this particular pit were rainbows. As the summer ended and the weather cooled off, the trout began to bite.

When I am hunting, I like to do the scouting and setup work myself. I do not spend any time grilling other hunters for tips on where to find a buck or a bunch of ducks; I get out and look around for them. With fishing, I am shameless. My two friends from work fished those mine pits regularly and, for whatever reason, they shared all of their information with me. Maybe it was because I was their boss. At any rate, when the reports of fast action got to me I quickly made a trip or two to this mine pit.

The most successful method these fellows had found for catching the rainbow trout in the pit was to fish in the evening and into the night using night crawlers. They used a bobber to suspend the worm six or so feet below the surface. They fished from shore, near the mouth of a stream that emptied into the pit. There was a public landing there and a nice grassy bank, free of trees, from which to fish. They had purchased bobbers with little lights in them that ran off a tiny battery, so I picked up a

couple of these myself. My boys came along with me a couple of times and other times I went alone. We would arrive an hour or so before dark and fish until the legal quitting time, which was 11:00 P.M. We would sit on the bank and let our bobbers drift along in the current from the little stream. Action was slow before dark, but as the sun dropped, the rainbows got aggressive.

It was late in the month. When the sun dipped below the horizon, there was a chill in the air that let you know autumn was on its way. A guy could get a little cold if the fish were not biting, but mostly they were.

The tiny, red lights on the bobbers were visible out on the water, the light being on the end of a sort of spike that stuck out of the body of the float. They were about three inches above the water, and you could see the reflection of the light on the water surface as well. When you had a nibble, the two little red dots started to get closer together as the fish pulled the bobber down. Often the dots merged into a single one, then faded as the fish pulled it down deep. The hook was set and if you set it right, you had a fight on your hands.

The rainbow we caught were from twelve to eighteen inches long, beautiful fish that put up a good battle. We did well. It made for a pleasant evening, sitting there in the cool night air with a gas lantern hissing and giving us just enough light to not trip over things. The little red lights of the bobbers added a neat touch to the outing.

One year, a bear was hanging around our fishing area. Some of the guys had seen it and one evening I could hear it wading back and forth across the little stream and splashing around in it.

We fished as late as the law allowed, then packed up and drove home. It was a sleepy ride for me and the boys were quickly asleep. I recall many such rides home when I was a boy, Dad at the wheel, listening to the Detroit Tiger baseball game. I would fall asleep with the smell of worms and fish all over me, tired and happy. I have a nice picture or two of my sons, holding a stick between them, weighed down by three limits of rainbow trout. Fifteen fish, from twelve to eighteen inches long. Their smiles tell the story.

There is one other memory from our fishing trips to the pit that stands out vividly. It would have to have been well after midnight when we arrived home. There were fish to clean. I sent the boys to bed and would take a chair, bucket, and whatever else I needed to gut the fish, and would set up under one of the yard lights. It was very cool. The foretelling of the autumn was in the air. My hands suffered a little from the cold while gutting the pile of fish. The skies were clear and the stars bright. As I worked, I listened to the calls of barred owls, and on occasion, a pack of coyotes. Like me, they are hunters. In just a few weeks, I would be joining them.

It had been a very long day, and I was so tired. It felt so good.

Four-Acre Pond

I have had a rather pleasant dilemma over the years regarding ponds. I build them on my land, you see, and over time, I have been fortunate to be able to regularly add more of them. The only problem with this is that the term "the new pond" can get confusing. We have Old Pond, and that description will not change. We have Big Pond, and although there are now bigger ones—built since—its name will not be changed even if it occasionally causes some confusion. That "new pond" description has referred to a different body of water every couple of years. In a previous chapter, I described the initial work we did over the winter on the "newest" pond project. After that phase, I had set up three wood duck boxes within the area of the planned impoundment. As summer dried out the landscape, it was time to complete the project. I decided to call this new wetland habitat Four-Acre Pond. It may keep that moniker or it may be changed by popular demand when we stumble onto a "natural" description that immediately identifies it. Perhaps something on the order of "Dan's Folly."

During the spring, ducks and geese had immediately explored the new habitat. To me, the newly dug trench—now holding a foot or two of water—seemed devoid of any vegetation or animal matter that would have provided food. Still, the birds seemed to be feeding here regularly. Perhaps the soil held old seeds or roots that were now exposed and available or maybe the invertebrates the birds relish were already populating the shallow water. At any rate, the birds put a stamp of approval on the project by early spring.

June and July quickly slipped behind us. The weather and the schedule of my contractor, Gerald Wick, allowed us to get back on task in August. I was getting financial assistance on the project from the Minnesota DNR. I had also applied to the Minnesota Waterfowl Association for additional aid. I finally received word that MWA had approved the project for funding by local chapters, but had only received a commitment from one of these local groups. Because we were running out of time to complete the project, it was necessary to proceed with a modified—and less costly—plan. I would eliminate one of the planned water control structures. This would limit my ability to closely control the water level in the impounded area, but it certainly would not render the four-acre wetland unacceptable for waterfowl. Near the end of the month, the excavator and dozer moved in.

While the professional equipment operators did their thing, I struggled with the manual labor. After years behind a desk, doing manual labor was almost like a vacation in some respects. However, in this case, I was racing against time. I needed to construct an emergency spillway to handle heavy runoff that might overwhelm the water level control device. The lay of the land is such that one heavy rain could turn the small ditch (that feeds this area) from a dry trench to a three-foot deep, fast-flowing stream. Without the spillway in place, such an event might wash away the dike. I had to complete the project in a day or two.

Gerald has a fine eye for running a dozer. I asked him to cut a "notch" in the dike that would be twenty-five feet long and eighteen inches lower than the top of the dike. We paced off the twenty-five foot length, and he lowered the blade and pushed away a slice of the deep, black, peaty soil. We placed the transit rod at the bottom of the notch and slid the top of it to a point where the laser sensor beeped at us. It was telling us it was now in touch with the laser generating transit mounted three hundred feet away. We did the math and the notch was within a fraction of an inch of the correct depth. How anyone could come so close from the driver's seat of that dozer is beyond me, but over and over, I have seen experienced equipment operators demonstrate such skill.

I used approximately fifty timbers to construct the spillway. Each was six feet long and measured six by eight inches. We lay them end-to-end in the notch, staggering five rows of them. Treated two by twelve lumber was then laid across the five rows of timbers in four places. Lag screws and spikes were used to tie the whole creation together and bags of concrete were stacked in several places to temporarily hold it in place should the water come up and try to float it away. Later, steel anchors were augured deep into the soil, two on the upstream side and two on the downstream side. Heavy chains were run across the wooden device and connected to the anchors. The spillway was pronounced finished.

After a rainy day caused a short interruption, the dozer was able to do a nice job of finishing off the dike and leveling off all the areas where earth had been pushed. I then got to play farmer.

Using my four-wheeler, I dragged a small spring-toothed harrow back and forth across the exposed earth. In some places, this was silty sand, in others it was dark, peaty soil. After the soil was worked up, I walked along with a small hand seeder, cranking the handle to spread rye, clover and orchard grass seed. Then, I pulled a large roll of chain link fence over the entire seeded area. The heavy roll of fencing was partially unrolled so perhaps ten feet of fencing trailed behind the heavy roll. It did a nice job of leveling and smoothing the dirt.

When the seeding was complete, the lower gates of the water control device were closed. We waited for rain and watched the banks take on a tint of green as the seed germinated, turning to a lush, bright green as the plants flourished in the fertile soil and open sunlight. The deer found the new growth and began their first tentative sampling of this new feeding ground. A blue heron began to hunt regularly in the shallows and a kingfisher began to stalk the minnows and tadpoles that already populated the shallow water. He moved from perch to perch on the ash trees that were left standing within the pond area, and I watched him swoop down and splash into the water many times, as he tried to

obtain a hard-earned meal.

The center portion of the pond was still not flooded. It was covered with weeds that had sprouted in the soil that was exposed when the initial clearing had been done on the site. Like most invasive weeds, they were loaded with seed, and songbirds descended on these in great numbers. When the fall rains came, this area would be flooded, and perhaps the ducks would begin to utilize this food source just as the songbirds were now doing.

One morning, as I drove the four-wheeler out to check on the new project, a young fox entertained me and gave me an opportunity to take his photo. It was obviously a youngster, very small, and not very wise. I drove to within thirty yards and stopped the machine as the animal innocently watched. It then retreated, but moved onto a small peninsula that reached out from the dike and was covered with brush left behind by the dozer. I had him cut off, and he would have to either come right by me or swim if he wanted to leave the peninsula. I squeaked with my mouth and got him to peek out from behind the brush at me. Finally, he scurried over the brush pile and dashed past me as I snapped one more photo.

The first significant rainfall did not come until the first week of October. An all-night rain was followed by a full day of the same. At mid-day, I donned my rain gear and walked out to look things over. From the time I had closed the gates on the control structure until the previous day, the water had come up perhaps one and one-half inches. Now another two inches of water had been added.

The next day was sunny, but the runoff from the surrounding landscape was now reaching the pond. It added another four inches of water, bringing the water level to within two inches of the top of the spillway. The center portion of the pond was now inundated by a shallow sheet of water, covering all but the highest areas. More rain arrived the following day, and the water began to creep across the spillway. I was pleased.

I watched all of these developments with great interest; I suppose just as a farmer watches his crop develop. Here was something I had dreamed up and then made happen. I knew what results I was hoping for, and I will watch Four-Acre Pond very closely over the next couple of years to see how the rice and arrowhead and other vegetation develops. I will check the duck boxes and watch for wildlife and their signs to learn which of my wild neighbors are benefiting from this new wetland. Just as I still watch similar projects, completed a dozen years ago. The lawn chair is in place, overlooking the new project, and it will be used often. Four-Acre Pond is one investment with a guaranteed return.

Anticipation

So much to do—so little time. For me, that has been the theme of August for many years. The summer is full. With weddings, reunions, and events of every description, hunting preparations are put aside in favor of other commitments. Now, in August, this hunter begins to realize how little time there is before the season is upon me. Maybe this year will be different. Most likely, it will not.

When the 2002 hunting seasons draws near, I will look back to 2001 and realize it will be almost impossible to capture again, in one season, the variety and quality of experience that was mine during that year. It is not that I see the upcoming year as being a let down or disappointing in any way. Rather it is a statement of how rewarding that season a year ago had been. What more could a guy ask for? I hunted in four states and hunted in ways and in places that were totally new experiences. I also hunted in a place that was very nostalgic and with people who I had not shared a camp with in three decades. As always, there were hunts in the familiar marshes and woodlands. Many were solitary hunts with only my dog. It is in these solitary hunts that I seem to find the most contentment, but the season would be a failure if it passed without some time afield with the many friends that share my interest.

Studies have been done—by those smart folk who study things—regarding hunters and their attitudes about the sport. These studies reveal that most hunters go through several stages that range from the beginner, who enjoys hearing his gun go off more than anything else, to the naturalist who is more concerned about the broad experience of the hunt and his close communion with nature. In between, there is a "limiting out" stage and a "trophy hunter" stage. My memory may be missing a stage or two here. The studies also show that you might be at one stage with your duck hunting (for example) and a different stage with your deer hunting. Most of us who hunt can see these stages in ourselves. I know that I do. I enjoy the sound of my beagle running a rabbit and would rather listen to a long chase than shoot the rabbit. However, I will shoot a few rabbits and have a good time doing it. Killing a rabbit this way is also a reward for the dog. That would put me at the naturalist stage with my rabbit hunting.

With my waterfowl hunting, I am slowly moving into the trophy hunter stage, passing up some hens now and again and looking to harvest new kinds of ducks I have never killed. My pintail drakes from Arkansas, along with the specklebelly and snow geese I took there, are certainly trophies in my eyes. More treasures from the 2001 season.

I think there is also a class of hunter I would call the "practical" hunter. This is the person who hunts more for the meat or fur than for the sport of it. When our area was full of farmers, there were many hunters of this type, those busy with farming and most likely struggling—like most farmers always seem to be—to pay the bills. The harvest of a deer was an important task. There are still many people who buy a deer license and are happy to take the first legal target that presents itself. They then hang up the gun for the year. Most of them enjoy the hunt too, and many are excellent hunters. They are practical and pragmatic hunters, and there is certainly nothing wrong with their approach. This fall, I hope to be a practical bear hunter. I have taken two bear with my bow and those hunts were definitely sport hunts. The meat was good and we used it all. In June, I drew a bear permit, as did my brother-in-law, Wes. This fall I will hunt bear but will use my rifle. I am interested in the expeditious acquisition of bear roast. In bear hunting, I am in the practical hunter stage.

Another plan rattling around inside my head is to expand my

trapping knowledge and experience. If the water in the West Branch is high enough come trapping season, and if I can borrow some traps big enough to handle beaver and otter, I may try it. The trap-line that I envision will run from Wawina to Cedar Valley along the river. It will include a campsite halfway through, for it will take two days to run the entire line. It will be a chore for this tired old body, but what an adventure this could be!

The rice crop in my ponds is sure to bring in some ducks, and the deer should be even more numerous than last year, given they had a very easy winter. Jake will see his first real action, and Jill will be at my side almost constantly. When the season is on, not only do Jill and I spend many hours afield together, but also when in the house, she sort of clings to me. I would like to flatter myself that she is drawn to me because I am taking her hunting every chance I get. However, it may just be that she is keeping an eye on me lest I try to leave the house without her. Whichever it is, I know when I move from place to place in the house she will follow and curl up near me whenever I sit down. When I reach over to scratch her she will sit up, tip her nose upward with eyes closed, and throw one paw over my arm as if to hold it there. If Jake sees this, he will gallop over and try to worm his nose in between my hand and Jill.

Until the season opens, I will prepare the gear, scout the game and work the dogs. I will look back on 2001 and the many seasons before it, remembering the many wonderful days this sport, this way of life, has given to me. The months to come have an uncertainty associated with them because of things unrelated to hunting. I will be trying to make my living in a new field, and there is much to learn. However, a few things are certain. The months just ahead will be the best part of the year. A hunter's year.

The End

The Author

Dan Prusi was born in Ishpeming, Michigan, in 1953. He grew up in and around nearby Negaunee, and graduated from Negaunee High School in 1971, moving to Minnesota in 1972. There he married Sherilee Tuominen in 1973. The couple resides in Cedar Valley Township, near Floodwood, Minnesota, and have three grown children.

An avid outdoorsman and amateur naturalist, Dan owns and resides on a seventy-seven acre property that is managed for wildlife. After a twenty-eight year career in the manufacturing world, he has turned to writing—a life-long hobby—as a second career.

Autographed copies of this and Dan Prusi's other books:

A Hunter's Journey - The Education of an Outdoorsman
and
Country Boy - Adventures from an Untroubled Childhood

may be ordered directly from the author. Contact him at:
TalesFromCV@aol.com
or
Box 482, Floodwood, MN 55736-0482.